The Politics of Curriculum Change

The Politics of Curriculum Change

Tony Becher & Stuart Maclure

Hutchinson of London

Hutchinson & Co (Publishers) Ltd
3 Fitzroy Square, London W1

London Melbourne Sydney Auckland
Wellington Johannesburg and agencies
throughout the world

First published 1978
© Tony Becher and Stuart Maclure 1978

Set in Monotype Imprint
Printed in Great Britain by The Anchor Press Ltd
and bound by Wm Brendon & Son Ltd
both of Tiptree, Essex

ISBN 0 09 132741 5

Contents

Acknowledgements

We are conscious of debts to many people over several years who have helped directly and indirectly, knowingly or unknowingly, to bring this book about. In particular our thanks are due to Geoffrey Caston, Robert Morris, Guy Neave, Joslyn Owen and Lawrence Stenhouse who read all or part of the text and made helpful comments; to Colin MacLean for guidance on Scottish practice reflected at the end of Chapter 3; and to Mrs Sue Major of Hutchinson who helped to prepare the final manuscript, responsibility for which, of course, is ours alone.

Our thanks are due to Her Majesty's Stationery Office for permission to quote paras 505–507 of the Plowdon report, *Children and their Primary Schools*.

Introduction

The ambiguous term 'curriculum development' still bears the tarnished brightness of novelty, conjuring up as it does the fashions of the 1960s when the impact of North American interest in educational innovation and curriculum reform began to be felt in Britain.

Within about fifteen years the curriculum development industry has grown up, and expanded out of recognition. Not only has there been the Schools Council for England and Wales, with its huge output of publications and projects, but also a growing concern with curricular studies in colleges and departments of education, and in in-service training. At the level of the individual school more and more teachers have wished to take a fresh look at what they are trying to do, and the package of activities through which they might do it.

This book is an attempt to sort out the variety of materials which make up the present patchwork of curriculum development. It is not suggested that everything can, or should, be reduced to a tidy symmetry – simply that without an overview it is more difficult to make sense of the individual parts. What is needed is to demystify curriculum development, to clarify its special demands and special skills, and to undermine the idea that it is a black art understood only by experts and initiates.

First we have to disentangle the confusion over the very concept of the curriculum – a confusion which is all too easily bequeathed to its development. We have to identify the various agents of development and control and how they are related. Here the experience of several education systems may usefully illustrate how the principles and practice of curriculum development grow out of the national educational context. We have to place the new-style post-Sputnik forms of development, with their paraphernalia of experimental models, field tests and feedback mechanisms, alongside the more familiar and traditional, if less highly organized, methods of curricular change.

It is then necessary to consider some of the important distinctions between system-based development – development of a system as a whole, including the curriculum – and subject-based development. These raise questions about the natural tendency of the curriculum to fragment, and the resulting quest for interdisciplinary studies and a unifying 'common core'. Dissemination and evaluation are also to be seen as integral parts of development.

The speech of the British Prime Minister, Mr James Callaghan, at Ruskin College, Oxford on 18 October 1976, gave a new urgency to curricular discussion. His intervention was more important for the change in official policy it signified than for the precise words he used. It marked a major change in the attitude of government towards the curriculum and the location of responsibility for the content of education. It called the bluff of the more extreme exponents of the teacher-controlled curriculum, and initiated a programme of consultations aimed at bringing the curriculum back into the public arena. In the course of time it has been followed by documents from Her Majesty's Inspectorate and the direct involvement of the Department of Education and Science in the reform of the secondary school examination system, with the express object of using this traditional control mechanism to influence the school curriculum.

It has not been our intention to try to guess how these developments will work out in the short term, but rather to underline the importance of all this for curriculum *development* as well as for curriculum control. It is our contention that, in many respects, the weakness of curriculum development in England and Wales in recent years has reflected the confusion about curricular aims and priorities to which Mr Callaghan drew attention. Without a sturdy framework of national policy it is not likely that local development, or any other kind of curriculum innovation, can make coherent sense.

A last word, by way of introduction, concerns differences of educational jurisdiction within the United Kingdom. Most of this book is about what happens in England and Wales, though the issues which are raised extend across frontiers and system boundaries. As everyone knows who has ever tried to describe 'British' education to someone from outside the British Isles, Scotland and Northern Ireland have their own education laws and administrative practice. A note on some aspects of the control and development of the curriculum in Scotland appears at the end of Chapter 3.

1 The curriculum and its development

What is curriculum?

To ask 'what is the curriculum?' is not simply to imitate the pedantic judge who displays his judicial ignorance to force counsel to define something everyone knows. The answer which is given stakes out the territory to which the curriculum developer lays claim.

Let us start with common parlance. The *Shorter Oxford Dictionary* is terse: '*Curriculum* pl. -ula. 1633 (L) A course.' When most people – teachers and laymen alike – talk about curriculum they start from some such narrow meaning as this. Quite commonly they use the term as if it were synonymous with syllabus. They may speak of the 'geography curriculum' or the 'science curriculum' – and they mean the specific content brought together and called a 'subject'. In a much-quoted article entitled 'A Glossary of Curriculum Terms'[1] W. F. Connell describes 'the Subject Curriculum':

(a) Certain bodies of subject matter are arranged in logical order to facilitate exposition and are called subjects.
(b) These subjects are determined in advance of the school lesson or pupil's learning experience.
(c) Teaching and learning are for the most part channelled into these already organised fields. This is the commonest form of curriculum.

Thus 'curriculum' is distinguished in common parlance not only from the school's organization, teaching methods, discipline and so on, but also from 'extra-curricular' activities; these it assumes to be different in kind.

We can call this the narrow meaning of the word. As a term to describe something of great everyday importance in professional and private conversation it is too useful to allow any amount of super-imposed jargon to swamp it as a general term for a specific aspect of education.

There are, however, equally powerful and practical reasons to use the word to describe something wider than subject content. Even the narrow meaning covers combinations of subjects which form themselves into recognizable patterns. It is a small, but important, step from this to the idea of 'the curriculum as a whole' – that is, more than just the aggregation of the syllabuses of the subject courses which are listed on a timetable.

When people speak of 'the school curriculum' or 'the curriculum of Greyfriars School' they include not only the available subject curricula but also all the other educational encounters – relating to personal relationships, moral attitudes, social habits and so forth – offered by the school. In this sense, in fact, the curriculum is as wide as the entire set of chosen activities by which the school seeks to achieve its educating purpose; it is 'what happens in school as a result of what teachers do . . . [the curriculum] includes all of the experiences of children for which the school accepts responsibility. It is the programme used by the school as a means of accomplishing its purpose.'[2] A string of such definitions are quoted in the textbooks.[3]

Too all-inclusive a definition, however, will be useless, as the Open University coursebook *Thinking about the Curriculum* recognizes.

What we shall do here is to offer a definition which can serve temporarily both as a starting point for our discussion and as a comfort for those who like to have precise statements as a guideline for their thinking. However, as you will find, we qualify this definition constantly as we develop our ideas. It is no catch-all definition by any means, and should never be regarded as such. Here it is: A curriculum is the offering of socially valued knowledge, skills and attitudes made available to students through a variety of arrangements during the time they are at school, college or university.[4]

All this goes a long way beyond the subject curriculum. It is certainly not what people usually mean when they complain about what Johnny does or doesn't learn at school. It amounts to saying that the school curriculum embraces many organized forms of learning beyond those prescribed (by state, l.e.a., school, teacher or examination board) for the learning of particular subjects and skills. It quickly ties up with other educational ideas about the aims of education – teaching Johnny as well as teaching Latin – and suggests, for example, that the prefect system may be as much part of the curriculum of a secondary school as, say, the set Shakespeare plays studied for the General Certificate of Education at Ordinary Level.[5]

It takes in so-called extra-curricular activities as part of the curriculum – that is, as part of the total planned activity of the school. Obviously, not all pupils follow the same programme even in the same teaching group or class. Some of the school's activities are common to all; but for the most part the curriculum consists of combinations of essential and optional programmes and activities, some chosen by the pupil for himself, others chosen for him by the school. In so far as it makes sense to talk in general terms about the curriculum of school X or school Y, this is a way of describing the mixture of individual curricula which the school offers and the process by which pupils are guided in the choices they have to make. Questions then arise about the internal organization of schools, the arrangements of year groups, promotion from one year to another, streaming, setting, examinations, the organization of separate schools into an articulated system, the teaching and learning methods prescribed, encouraged or expected.

This broad definition raises as many questions as it answers. It comes perilously close to making 'curriculum' synonymous with 'education'. But in so doing it merely reflects the complexity of the educational instruments deployed by schools and teachers. What it does do is reject the restricted view of the educational process which a discussion of courses and syllabuses only would convey.

For the curriculum developer the broad definition is important for three reasons. First, his terms of reference have to be correspondingly wide. His aim is to improve the education which the pupil actually receives. If he confines himself to the design of syllabuses and work schemes he is neglecting a wide range of curricular influences. It is true that for a variety of reasons a great deal of curriculum development in recent years has erred in just this way.

Secondly, the work of curriculum development is not completed till it has actually penetrated the classroom and influenced what goes on between individual teachers and individual learners. This implication, too, has been neglected in much of the best-known development work of recent years.

Finally, curriculum development has to be regarded as the responsibility of a much wider group of people than those specialists conventionally described as curriculum developers; in fact we must reject the narrow technical basis of many recent curriculum development projects on both sides of the Atlantic and make sure that the development process is seen in a much broader pedagogic setting.

Anglo-Saxon and Continental

Broadening the definition of the term curriculum highlights the differences in educational philosophy between different educational traditions. The French and Germans use no direct translation of the term. The French *programme et méthode* covers the narrow meaning adequately, but it is an Anglo-Saxon characteristic to insist that pupils in school must learn more than a blinkered look at the subject timetable might imply – though the form this has taken has been different on opposite sides of the Atlantic.

The philosophic background to the French approach explains the contrast in attitude. Traditionally the French have given the highest priority to *instruction* as the main function of the school. If, on Platonic reasoning, no man does wrong knowingly, it is from ignorance that 'evil' stems. Schools can, therefore, best promote 'virtue' by imparting knowledge and skill. *Education*, on the other hand, they have regarded as the larger, less precise business of upbringing in which many persons and agencies share – the family, the church, the community at large. French tradition therefore sees it as enough that pupils in school should be properly taught a body of knowledge and range of skills which form the intellectual and practical equipment for the educated individual. On this view, syllabus content and teaching methods can be laid down in more or less detail by a central authority and teachers play their parts within the limits of the role implied. As in England, religious controversy helped to form the tradition: attempts at moral training or character-building by schools might endanger the basic principle of *laïcité* which is engraved on the tablets of French education law, and thus invade the prerogative of others. This traditional view has been much modified; for example, *enseignement* now tends to replace *instruction* in French education jargon, while there is a greater willingness to speak of *education* as a proper function of schooling. (The Ministry of Public Instruction became the Ministry of Public Education by 1932 – the word Public being dropped in 1974.) In a real sense, however, the educational tradition is still rooted in the ideas expressed by the earlier terminology.

By contrast Anglo-Saxon attitudes reflect an Aristotelian interest in the moral purposes of education whose object, Aristotle asserted, is to 'cause us to like and dislike what we ought to'. Limiting education to its intellectual content, then, would be to neglect that weakness of will which, unfortunately, prevents knowledge from always being fulfilled in virtue; other forms of moral training, other exercises in the schooling of the will and the affections, must be as or more important. Hence, in extreme form, the British public school in the later nineteenth century and after, which valued character above learning and made this scale of priorities operational by endowing prefects and sportsmen with power and prestige. The same attitudes could be discerned in the Oxford and Cambridge of that time.

Nor did anyone think the working-class elementary schools' aims to be adequately summed up in the examinable standards I–VII laid down by the Elementary Code. True, the Revised Code was narrow in the range of knowledge included in the 'standards' which pupils were expected to reach, but it never implied secular instruction was all that mattered, simply that the Three Rs provided a measurable criterion for the allocation of government grants.[6] A nineteenth-century commentator might have baulked at including the school's moral and character-moulding aims within his narrow definition of the 'curriculum' but they would certainly have been of paramount importance to him.[7] It was assumed that moral duties were distributed in different ways to different social classes, but the importance of this kind of non-cognitive learning was recognized as clearly by the head of an elementary school as by Dr Arnold.

It can easily be seen that such a view of education would not march happily with a centrally designed curriculum – except in a totalitarian country with an all-pervasive ideology – because it assumes that the individual teacher takes on the role of moral guide and exemplar for his pupils, as well as simply purveying the technique of a given academic discipline. 'The freedom of the teacher' (that most beguiling of all half-truths about the English educational system) is linked to this ideal of educational virtue, caught as much as taught, in which the individual teacher must be allowed a wide latitude in modifying and interpreting the public curriculum for 'his' pupils.

Many teachers have themselves been much more interested in helping their pupils to develop and realize their potential as people than in simply imparting to them knowledge and skills. Their aims, as teachers, and the satisfaction which they have got from their jobs, have been tied up with these larger concerns, around which they have built a tradition of education in which particular value has been set on the school as a community. But if in such a community it is important to build 'character' and train morals (real or imagined), through physical activity or through social responsibility exercised on behalf of the school, then 'instruction' in school 'subjects' comes to be seen as only a part, perhaps not first in importance, of the school's curriculum. Changes in teaching methods and in the significance attached to motivation have extended recognition of the range of experience a school lays before its pupils, and on this view of the curriculum a school bears as its responsibility the whole moral, intellectual, emotional and social development of the pupil.[8]

The public curriculum

Having stressed the importance of the broad definition and indicated some of its educational implications, we are left with the idea of curriculum as some huge, amorphous totality. Something more manageable is needed. The actual curriculum experienced by the pupil, to which the separate decisions of many independent individuals may contribute, is elusive and difficult to describe in advance. At times it must seem that the most you can say is – retrospectively – 'that's the curriculum, that was'.

A more restricted term must assert two necessary ideas. The first is that the curriculum embodies rational intentions – it is a means to an end, even if the end is not analysed with any rigour, and is usually taken for granted within the familiar dimensions of an educational tradition. The second is that, as a social phenomenon, the curriculum is not to be regarded as so individual as to be devoid of any collective intent: there are, in fact, aspects of the curriculum which are intended to be shared, and about which collective decisions have to be taken.

This introduces the idea of a *public curriculum*. By this we mean those aspects of the curriculum which embody an education system's shared assumptions, however formulated, about the main things which pupils should do and learn at school. In the next chapter there is a discussion of the mechanisms by which the public curriculum has been controlled and how these control mechanisms are related to the institutions which are concerned with curriculum development and change. At one extreme stand the Scandinavian countries, where the curriculum is written down in large printed volumes, and distributed to each school with the compliments of the central government's education department. At the other stands the informal technique practised in England and Wales where the guidelines are laid down by employers and their recruitment needs; by examination boards and university admissions officers and educational publishers;

by a wide range of administrative decisions taken by central and local government (many of which are not generally recognized as curricular decisions at all); by the activities of school inspectors and advisors; and by the powerful educational tradition which conditions the way in which individual teachers exercise their limited but undeniable freedom.

The theory, at least, of the public curriculum makes the assertion that education is not just a private matter but one in which society is entitled to take a hand. The administrative means by which these social requirements are established may differ widely in the degrees to which they are open, efficient and well researched. But establishing society's educational demands is a political act; it cannot be regarded as a purely professional operation.

In England the public nature of the curriculum has been concealed by the way its control is shared among a variety of autonomous and semi-autonomous bodies. Most obviously has this been true of the role of the Secretary of State for Education and Science, who has residual responsibility for examinations. By the mid-1970s this had become a matter of warm debate, and the time was ripe for change. But for many years, successive ministers had striven to avoid expressing any views – let alone taking any decision – about the curricular questions with which the examination boards deal. Instead they encouraged the 'professionalization' of the curriculum by leaving the discussion of examination questions to advisory councils dominated by professionals. Professionals and laymen alike have joined in keeping the public curriculum away from any public forum or debate. This is a theme to which we shall return in Chapter 10.

Beyond the public curriculum

If the public curriculum were all, then the processes of curriculum development, though difficult and cumbersome because of the legislative or administrative law-making involved in bringing about any change, would be relatively simple to understand. It would be sufficient to discover where formal control is located and then, by authoritarian or democratic methods, to use the formal control mechanism to initiate change.

But – and this is where the broad definition of curriculum, and the broad concept of what education is all about, again become important – the public curriculum is not by any means the whole of the story. There is, in fact, a gap between the public curriculum and the actual regime under which children live and learn at school.

In England this is the professional inheritance and pride of the teacher and a valuable myth has grown up around it – valuable in the sense that many good things can the more easily happen because of it. But it is by no means the exclusive preserve of teachers in England and Wales. Under no educational system can the professional relationship between teacher and child be wholly constrained by a predetermined set of propositions laid down in advance by an outside authority. This is true whether or not the public curriculum is the subject of public debate and parliamentary control, or under the authority of a powerful educational administration. Systems which the British in their ignorance cheerfully dub authoritarian and centrally controlled almost invariably recognize this: much of the public curriculum in, say, Norway or Sweden depends on advice (not direction) conveyed in different forms by one group of people in the education system to another. It may or may not be backed up with sanctions; it may be detailed or vague, conventionally obeyed or disregarded. It may multiply till one control begins to cancel out another. But whatever else it may do, it does not eliminate the gap between the public curriculum and what actually happens at the classroom level.

Lawrence Stenhouse[9] has likened the public curriculum to a child's colouring book – a set of outlines which have to be filled in by the only people who are in a position to do so, the teachers and pupils in the schools. Any concept of development which stops short at the public curriculum must be woefully inadequate; any real development must reach the actual page of the colouring book and the resources which the teachers bring to the task of painting in the outlines. 'The curriculum problem', as Stenhouse 'most simply and directly' states it, is that of 'relating ideas to realities, the curriculum in the mind or on paper to the curriculum in the classroom'.

What is curriculum development?

If the curriculum is as wide as everything that happens in school as a result of what teachers do, then we cannot confine the term curriculum development to specific attempts to reform subject content and introduce new teaching methods. Many different activities of government, education ministry, local education authority and individual school help to shape the curriculum, as do the activities of others outside the line management of the education system (for instance examining boards, publishing houses and the Schools Council for the Curriculum and Examinations); within all these there must be scope for curriculum development.

Some of these activities bring about curriculum change as a matter of routine maintenance. For example, let us suppose French is being taught according to certain well-tried syllabuses, by teachers who share a common training and a common set of standards to aim at. Within these conventions, new textbooks are written and marketed which seem to do the conventional job better. A few modest changes will from time to time be incorporated within the existing conventions and the examination arrangements may be adjusted in minor ways to take account of them. Meanwhile the teacher-education institutions initiate new generations of teachers into the business of teaching this French curriculum and the Inspectorate and local advisory services provide refresher courses and similar support. The chief aim is to maintain and improve standards of modern language teaching within the existing conventions.

Much change has in the past been a result of what Eric Hoyle calls 'relatively unplanned and adaptive "drift"'.[10] A few teachers in one school or group of schools may begin to flirt with some innovation of their own devising. They may decide that it would be best for their pupils if the order in which particular operations were approached were changed; or they may, because they have come to value different kinds of skill or insight, make deliberate changes in the content of study or the methods used to present it. By personal contact, their example may then spread gradually to other groups of teachers, leading in time to the production of a new book or series of books which might come to exercise a seminal influence among their professional colleagues and in institutions for teacher education. In the end, to be effective, their work might have to lead to an extension of the range of examination options.

Maintenance and evolution should be distinguished from development, a term which connotes system and rationality addressed to the task of positive improvement (whatever improvement may be thought to be). It involves some more general debate followed by some institutional efforts to encourage movement in a particular direction. The same agencies which are involved in curriculum maintenance may also be called in to the curriculum development process – but this time for the purpose of promoting and refining particular forms of innovative action. On other occasions, the curriculum development process may begin by trying to discover how practice is evolving and then go on to seek institutional ways (which may or may not require the production of teaching materials) to spread the evolutionary idea more efficiently and collect evidence of its merits or demerits in practice.

While such distinctions may be helpful at the conceptual level, the practical realities are less tidy. The ways in which the curriculum has traditionally been maintained, or has changed by a process of drift, are closely intertwined with the ways in which it has been developed. Although over-precise definition is therefore beside the point, three fairly simple criteria have been put forward[11] in an attempt to sketch some of the main characteristics of curriculum development. First, it must be institutionalized, at least to some extent; secondly, it must be a process of change intended to lead to improvement, and must include an element of feedback and evaluation (taking a broad interpretation of these); and, thirdly, it must be capable of being described in relation to the actual practice of school and classroom.

These criteria allow development to embrace a range of different activities, each of which in its own way attempts to offer some rational means of changing the curriculum, or parts of it, for what is deemed to be the better.

Such a wide interpretation of curriculum development disposes of the simplistic and unhistorical notion that curriculum development is something peculiar to the second half of the twentieth century – a by-product of the space age and systems engineering. It is true that a particular type of development, which we shall label *heuristic*, originated in the late 1950s, and that many of the institutions which now regard themselves as the main repositories of conventional wisdom on this subject date from this period in the United States and from the following decade in Britain, Scandinavia and the rest of Europe. But in reality, far from being something invented by the Americans in the immediate post-Sputnik era, curriculum development in what might be described as its *traditional* form has taken place for as long as the educational system has existed.

2 A European perspective

The way different countries decide to organize curriculum development is closely related to the way in which they administer education
generally: where development functions are located, and to whom
they are entrusted, depends less on theories about the management
of innovation than on the legal and administrative instruments of
curriculum control.[1]

Where the school curriculum is laid down centrally (whether by
the state, province, local authority or school board) the formal
document setting down the official programme may go into considerable detail (as in Norway and Sweden) or be limited to an outline
syllabus (as in some of the German *Länder*). It will usually specify
the number of timetable hours to be devoted to each subject, and it
may, as in Scandinavia and lately in France, deliberately provide for
a limited period of the week to be at the elective disposal of the school
or the local school board. It may prescribe the textbooks and other
teaching materials or set down a list of approved books and teaching
aids from which schools can choose. Individual school boards or
local authorities may be further constrained by costs, especially if
financial responsibility is divided between central and local government, so that teachers' salaries, say, are a charge on central government while books and equipment have to be paid for out of local
funds.

Entrance to higher education is usually through a system of
examination or grading by teachers at the end of the secondary
school; even if it is administered internally by the school this too
may control the curriculum. If entry to more favoured faculties
and institutions is competitive, parents and the local community will
exert conservative pressures.

Scandinavia

Though they differ in emphasis and practice, Finland, Norway and

Sweden share a common approach to educational administration and curriculum development. In the first place, they all see curriculum development as an integral part of a larger policy of educational reform.[2] The social and political objectives of this educational reform are determined by Parliament: they, in their turn, are part of a larger policy for the transformation of society as a whole.

Objectives are therefore outside the development process (though it may cause them to be refined in particular respects from time to time). On the other hand, changes in the internal organization of the school or of the framework of relationships within which the school operates are closely connected with curriculum development: hence in Sweden,[3] for instance, a concern to study all the 'frame factors' affecting a child's learning and social development; hence also a government commission (the SIA Commission) on the internal organization of schools which, while not nominally about curriculum development, was immediately involved in many of the matters which concern curriculum developers.

All three countries have a system of curriculum guidance which leads to the production of very full documents which are sent to individual schools and which constitute for them the public curriculum. In Finland inspectors are employed to supervise the application of this public curriculum. Schools can expect to be inspected one year in three. In Norway and Sweden there are differences in the degree of detail in the different parts of the *Mønsterplan* or the *Läroplan*, and differences, too, in the extent to which teachers feel bound by them. Some sections of the Swedish *Läroplan* have parliamentary authority and are mandatory upon the schools; others are advisory, expressing the conventional wisdom of the élite group of teachers on whom the National Board of Education rely. No doubt teachers find scope within the copious handbooks for selective quotation to support those aspects of official policy they prefer. Through the published curriculum documents changes in the curriculum are, as it were, formally registered and transmitted to the schools. This would be so even were there no formal methods of curriculum development, as opposed to curriculum change.

Development is thus one of the functions of the government department responsible for the administration of the schools. In Finland the Experiment and Research Office is an integral part of the National Board of Schools, calling on the Institute of Educational Research at the University of Tyvaskyla when evaluation is required. In Norway the National Council for Innovation in Education

(NCIE) is a separate administrative structure, affiliated to the Norwegian Education Ministry, which is responsible for approved experimental and innovative developments which the Ministry's regulations would not otherwise allow.[4] When and if an experiment or an innovation graduates to the status of an established practice, the ordinary regulations are revised to accommodate it and the first stage of the process of development is complete. It was in this way that the organizational and curricular changes involved in the introduction of the comprehensive school were undertaken.

Such a system has naturally given rise to certain tensions between the NCIE and the rest of the Norwegian Ministry – for example, attempts to innovate in the upper secondary school were not always happily resolved by the Council for Upper Secondary Schools, the traditional arbiters of secondary school policy (ex-teachers, now Ministry officials, selected by the Minister). But the system has the merit of institutionalizing these tensions and permitting movement to take place piecemeal, a useful device if the strain of wholesale change is great.

Sweden's National Board supervises the curriculum at every level and its bureau for research and development directs much of its programme of investigation into the curriculum, using sophisticated social-science-based studies to translate the larger aims into specific objectives of school subjects. Projects designed to lead to the production of new curriculum materials (for example IMU mathematics)[5] are therefore inextricably linked with the National Board's administrative techniques, but they are not necessarily the 'typical' Swedish method; alongside is the more established process of formulating new syllabuses by simply assembling views – of inspectors on short-term attachment, of employers and trade unionists, of teachers and of academic observers. In-service training of teachers is closely linked to this – though not by any means only to this.

In Sweden and Norway alike recurrent, systematic consideration leads to the publication of the curriculum brief in the shape of the *Mønsterplan* and the *Läroplan*, and publishers are as concerned as teachers to analyse it. They then seek authors to prepare attractive and popular textbooks in conformity with it, and another round of curriculum development takes place on traditional lines.

In a recent attempt to decentralize some curriculum development activity the Swedish National Board and local school boards have jointly set up 'development blocks' within groups of schools, supported by a team from a university or college of education, which test new methods, new materials, new ways of deploying time and resources. The block aims to spread the best practice by example, by staff movement and by the proselytizing work of inspectors and consultants. The expectation is that suitable materials will appear in due course as publishers recognize changes in school practice and note market demands.

By their direct involvement of teachers in the process of development and by their concern with dissemination and implementation these Swedish 'development blocks' try to bridge the gap between the public curriculum and what teachers and their pupils actually pursue. They are not exclusively concerned with the curriculum as narrowly defined.

There is also an interest in decentralization in Norway, where the fact that there are no central government school inspectors in itself means that the 'public' curriculum is not closely policed.

The characteristics of Scandinavian curriculum development are summed up in the comparative table at the end of this chapter. Perhaps, however, we should not be too tidy-minded. One Norwegian curriculum expert has written:

> There is some lip-service in the Northern countries to the idea that educational reform should serve the purpose of changing society, maybe most marked in Sweden. Yet, looking at what really happens to the curriculum in this process, I think the most one can say is that there is an attempt to correct some of the most obvious biases inherited from the past, in order to reduce somewhat the distance between reality as conceived by most people today, and the picture of reality provided by the school. There is a long way to go even to cope with the task of catching up.
>
> Many of us would like to be radical, but the relatively few instances of genuine radicalism in the Scandinavian school systems are nearly always locally inspired, and somewhat embarrassing for the 'middle of the road' policy followed by official authorities. In an international comparison, this may of course be something, but too much emphasis on the 'changing society' policies of the Scandinavian countries could be rather misleading.

This is another way of dramatizing the gap between ideal and reality. But by comparison with many other countries, the strength of the social orientation of education in Norway and Sweden cannot be denied, and though the theory is not fully translated into practice, the systems in both countries clearly reflect the efforts made to this end.

France, Belgium, Austria and Spain

A second group of countries can be identified which have certain characteristics in common. Again, the limits of generalization are quickly reached: it is not suggested that their education systems or the societies they serve are without important differences which affect curriculum development. In some of these countries self-conscious developmental activities are only in their infancy. In France, on the other hand, a sophisticated organization exists, staffed by a cadre of highly trained inspectors who have strong ideas about how the curriculum should develop and clearly defined administrative techniques to carry out these ideas.

The overall control of the school curriculum in France lies firmly with the Minister of Education. The national curriculum guidelines in each subject are drafted by a series of curriculum commissions, which now include (beside the specialist administrative staff and the Inspecteurs Généraux themselves) selected senior teachers and – in the case of upper secondary curricula – subject specialists from universities. The draft guidelines are referred for informal consultation to relevant interest groups such as teachers' and parents' associations: but once endorsed, they are binding on all schools in the public sector. They include specifications of content to be taught, recommended teaching methods and approaches, and the time to be allowed in the school's weekly timetable.

This bald description makes the system of curriculum control sound more rigid than it is in practice. There is certainly no truth in the *canard* that, at any given moment, the Minister of Education will know precisely which grade of pupils all over France will have reached which particular page in which standard textbook. The French, besides their reputation for Cartesian logic, have another (and contrasting) reputation as a nation of confirmed individualists. So, while the overall curricular pattern is expected to be adhered to in general terms, there is room in practice for a good deal of individual variation in style from school to school and teacher to teacher.

Curriculum development, however, is not readily distinguishable from curriculum specification and control. Development normally takes place at national level through the work of the specialist curriculum commissions, in the form of periodic revisions to the guidelines published for each sector of the system and for each subject. But the commissions themselves are not impervious to outside forces: it is always possible for an active pressure group (such as the syndicate of mathematics teachers), or even an active and influential individual, to bring about an eventual change in the way a subject is taught.

But since in France the educational system is indissolubly bound up with the political system, any organized attempt to modify the status quo is liable to get caught up in political controversy. Many of the movements for educational reform are seen as having left-wing affiliations: if the Minister shows too much sympathy with them, he is attacked on his right flank. On the other hand, if he proceeds on his own initiative, the innovative-minded teachers see this as an incursion on their jealously guarded autonomy. Although there are numerous pressures for change, they stem from diverse and conflicting ideologies, and tend to be cancelled out by the pressures of conservatism.

Meanwhile, it is generally agreed that the schools are in a state of critical inertia, and that attempts have somehow to be made to work out a new structure within which educational researchers, policy-makers and teachers can work together to achieve agreed ends. A first step towards this new structure was taken in 1970, when the INRDP (Institut Nationale de Recherche et Documentation Pédagogique), the main official agency for curricular and other innovation, was formed (together with OFRATEME, the national organization for educational technology) out of the subdivision of the Institut Pédagogique Nationale. Its main function was research and documentation of a descriptive or evaluative kind: in this it collaborated with university-based research teams as well as with the administration and the Inspectorate. It also took a more active, developmental role, especially in connection with the major organizational reforms of the primary and the early secondary stages. A more recent reorganization has, however, had the effect of restoring the status quo, by reconstituting the IPN and eliminating its subsidiaries as separate entities.

The main challenges to national curricular assumptions come from the strong, and growing, private sector, or from 'grass roots' consortia of state schools organized on a local or national basis – of which the long-established group of Freinet schools provides the most striking example.[6] But, as in the Scandinavian group of countries, there is now a move away from immediate implementation of change on a nation-wide basis (where the consequences of any major decisions are so momentous that all but the most politically courageous of education ministers will shrink from taking them) to a more cautious and piecemeal approach. Thus, the central innovation agency is associated with a network of Centres Régionaux de Documentation Pédagogique, and with the evaluation of a number of pilot experiments in individual schools or experimental regions, as well as with the detailed implementation of reforms on a national scale.

For the most part, however, the task of spelling out national curricular guidelines in detailed classroom terms is left to the textbook publishers and their commissioned authors (usually experienced teachers, including some of those who serve on the relevant curriculum commissions). Teamwork in preparing curricular materials is still relatively rare, and draft publications are rarely tried out and then revised in the light of systematically collected classroom experience.

There is – in contrast to the other countries in this group – no central list of 'approved texts' but, because the regional inspectorate must approve each school's programme, textbook publishers and authors adhere closely to the spirit of the ministerial decrees. Indeed, these decrees are more studiously scanned by educational publishers than by teachers themselves, whose main concern is usually with the requirements laid down for the annual school examinations rather than with the curriculum itself. The average classroom teacher, although in theory free to develop his own approach within the framework provided by the national curricular guidelines, is usually content to accept the pattern worked out in one of the standard textbooks.[7]

Concern has now arisen at the lack of an active and critical force for curriculum reform within the teaching profession, and there is a move towards greater devolution of responsibility from the Ministry at the core of the system to the teachers at its operating surface. Examples of this are the increased allowance of discretionary time within the weekly timetable and the accompanying growth of interest at the Ministry in initial and in-service training provision.

The situation in Belgium is closely similar to that in France, since the two countries share many of the same cultural traditions. The issues here are complicated by the language divide, which results in two virtually separate systems, the Flemish and the Walloon, existing side by side. But apart from the Catholic schools – which form the large majority of the state-supported 'free school' sector, and enjoy a certain measure of freedom for curricular experiment within the limitations of the state requirements for examinations –

the educational provision is reasonably uniform between the two language groups. Comprehensive reorganization has been slower to take root here than in many other European systems, and the teaching profession as a whole seems to have taken a relatively inactive part in planned curriculum change.

This is not altogether surprising, given that the traditional philosophy – a purer version of its French counterpart – holds the only worthwhile development to be that undertaken by the individual teacher. The curricular guidelines having been set by central committees of experts, the teacher is expected to adapt them to his or her personal interests and the needs of his or her own students. So every piece of curriculum innovation is by definition *ad hoc*, dependent on a particular context, and hence unique. In accordance with this tradition there is little systematic attempt by Belgian educationalists (many of whom are of international standing) to undertake curricular research and development. There are no equivalents to the French regional centres or experimental schools.

A major reform – related to the move to introduce a common curriculum at the early secondary stage so as to defer selection by levels of academic ability – has been sponsored by the Central Reform Commission of the Ministry for French-speaking schools, chaired by the Minister himself or his chosen nominee. This programme, in which schools enlisted on a voluntary basis, was designed to encourage schools to take increasing responsibility for determining their own curricula. Another reform, initiated by the Ministry for Flemish-speaking schools, has concentrated on major changes in primary education. This programme, steered by a twelve-man commission (including inspectors and representative teachers from Catholic, state and municipal primary schools), has tried out and evaluated a variety of different teaching approaches in schools in four different regions of the country. Major reforms of curricula for individual subjects have stemmed from active academics and lively teacher associations in mathematics and modern languages.

Austria and Spain came later to the business of systematic curriculum development. In both countries, as in France and Belgium, the overall responsibility for defining the school curriculum rests with the Ministry of Education, which also controls the allocation of resources and authorizes the textbooks and teaching materials which may be used by teachers in following the national curriculum guidelines.

In Spain some measure of decentralization had already been

introduced under Franco by setting up institutes for educational study (ICEs) in a number of universities. The task of the ICEs is twofold: to provide in-service training for teachers and to develop prototype curriculum materials. Attempts to reorientate the curriculum of the 'basic school' (giving greater emphasis to social goals and to the development of expressive and creative abilities), and to introduce more integrated secondary curricula in science and social studies, were in their early stages when the regime altered. Events have moved and are moving swiftly in post-Franco Spain, and the schools and teacher-training institutions are likely to be among the social institutions most affected by the need to adjust to a new and democratic regime. If so, it would be reasonable to expect the pace of change to outstrip the capacity of curriculum development institutions.

Innovation in Austria is mainly through the Ministry's Centre for School Experiments and School Development, set up on the recommendation of a School Reform Committee appointed in 1969. The Centre began by concentrating its attention on a comparative study of comprehensive and traditional forms of school organization. This study involved the development of materials to support the teaching of German, English and mathematics for pupils with a comprehensive range of abilities. The Ministry has also carried out a project to specify in more detail the objectives of vocational secondary education. The Klagenfurt Institute of Educational Sciences (an institute of higher education) was established partly with a view to serving as a major innovative agency. The majority of the teaching profession, however, have so far had little incentive to play an effective part in organized curriculum change.

West Germany and the Netherlands

Clear national characteristics are less easily identifiable in West Germany and the Netherlands. In the Netherlands a theoretically uniform national system is fragmented and weakened by strong religious and political divergences among the schools themselves, while each of the West German *Länder* has its own educational system, organized along lines somewhat similar to those of Austria, France, Belgium and Spain.

Although the policies of the different *Länder* are to some extent harmonized by the Joint Conference of Ministers of Culture, they vary from one another in several important points of detail. For example, Hessen and the city-states of Berlin and Hamburg are politically committed to the comprehensive reorganization of secondary schools; the other *Länder* are either equivocal or firmly opposed to such changes. Each state ministry issues its own set of curriculum guidelines, some allowing relatively wide discretion to teachers, others permitting much less.

Special agencies for research into curriculum or other innovations abound: some free-standing and supported by a mixture of Federal, state and private funds; some based on universities; and some more directly under state ministry control. In many such institutes, the creation of academic theories is given greater emphasis than the conduct of practical experimentation. The fierce suspicion shown by the *Länder* towards any form of Federal intervention in education limits the influence of the *Bund* (Federal) Ministry largely – as in the USA – to the injection of additional funds to promote such innovations as may attract political or professional favour at the national level. The amount of central funding has been substantial and steadily increasing, though restricted by the rule that each allocation has to be matched on a 50–50 basis by the *Länd*-ministry concerned. Nevertheless, a sizeable number of development agencies, experimental schools and individual curriculum programmes have been funded in this way.

The high respect traditionally accorded by Germans to academic research inhibits the large majority of teachers from direct participation in the development process. Anyone wishing to embark on curriculum change feels obliged first to pick a way through the dense and luxuriant forest of theoretical speculation – and this seems to deter all but the most determined explorers.

Coupled with the inherent discouragement to any 'grass roots' development is the growing recognition on the part of state curriculum agencies that such development may gradually erode their power. Although a UNESCO Institute survey in the early 1970s identified well over a hundred schemes of development of various kinds and a few local groups have managed to survive, there have also been signs of disenchantment in West Germany with curriculum development. Perhaps many enterprises were set up on too small a scale to achieve an effective 'critical mass', while others embraced with excessive enthusiasm the notion of 'teacher-proof' curriculum materials. In any event, the backlash has taken the form (almost certainly over-idealistic, given a national tradition in which teachers have little experience of freedom in curricular decision-making) of a vogue for open-ended, school-based experimentation supported by a new structure of local teachers' centres. One positive consequence of this change of fashion is a greater concentration than in the past on schemes for the professional development of teachers, both pre-service and in-service. The attendant risk may be that it comes to be regarded as an adequate substitute for any critical attention to the curriculum itself, or to the creation of learning materials other than those already produced by one or two enterprising and efficient publishers on the basis of a series of centrally prescribed state guidelines. The political impossibility of setting up any national co-ordinating and sponsoring agency for curriculum development may aggravate this tendency.

In the Netherlands the national Ministry of Education – unlike that in England and Wales – issues general curriculum guidelines, albeit of a rather broad and permissive kind. It also centralizes, through the Inspectorate and the official testing agency, CITO, the national system of school-leaving examinations. But the tradition of teacher autonomy is strongly entrenched, and the profusion of different curriculum agencies (subject-based national curriculum reform committees, separate national pedagogical centres for Protestant, Catholic and state schools, the national agency for educational research, the new regional pedagogical centres, and various university-based development teams) ensures that no one voice dominates the babel of developmental activity. When, in addition, it is remembered that the schools are divided at both the primary and secondary levels into three separate networks (state or municipal, Catholic and Protestant), and further subdivided at the secondary level into vocational, normal and academic sectors, it is scarcely surprising that curricular decision-making tends to become somewhat diffused. The main financial sponsor of curriculum development is the Ministry of Education, a body which tends to respond to initiatives within the system rather than to take them itself. The influential primary mathematics programme WISKOBAS, established in 1968 and based on the Institute for the Development of Mathematical Instruction at Utrecht (which was in turn initiated by active teachers and academics on the mathematics reform commission), provides one example of an officially funded but semi-autonomous development. The more recent projects in secondary school biology and physics – again deriving from the reform commissions in those subjects – offer further instances. (The physics project, initiated in the autumn of 1972, was in fact

Table I Some differing national approaches to curriculum development

Dimensions affecting style	Scandinavia	France, Belgium, Austria and Spain	W. Germany and the Netherlands
1 Clarity of national aims of education	There is a clear framework of socio-political aims for system reform, including educational reform.	The social and political aims of education, while broadly based, are not clearly defined.	Multiple goals exist for educational reform. There is no clear consensus or nationally defined policy on educational aims.
2 Relationship of curriculum development to socio-political reform	Curriculum development is seen as a product of social and system-wide educational reform.	Curriculum development is seen as a product of social and educational reform.	Curriculum development is seen as a stimulus to educational reform rather than as a product of it.
3 Arena for control of curriculum policy	Curriculum policy is determined within a central government department as part of the comprehensive control of the education system. Clear objectives of reform are determined at central-government level.	Curriculum policy is determined within central government as an integral part of system-wide educational planning, but the connection between educational and social reform is not easy to discern.	The control of curriculum-policy formation is dispersed from central government to multiple agencies, including universities, examination boards, local education authorities and schools.
4 Arena for control of curriculum development	Curriculum development is controlled by a central government department which also has control of curriculum-policy formation.	Curriculum development takes place within a central government department, which also has control of the curriculum through the specification of syllabuses	Control of curriculum development is dispersed throughout the system, residing in multiple institutions, independent or quasi-independent from

	...and the control of examinations.		*central government in terms of policy, but dependent on central and local government and foundations for resources.*
5 Methods of curriculum development	Curriculum developers employ a mixture of *a priori* reasoning, negotiation, bargaining and heuristic methods.	There is less emphasis on heuristic methods than on the traditional approaches of *a priori* reasoning and the collective work of experienced people. Textbook publishers play an important part in curriculum development, basing their work on centrally published syllabuses.	Traditional and heuristic methods of curriculum development operate side by side, with relatively greater emphasis on heuristic methods.
6 Degree of decentralization	Little decentralization exists, but the need for it is now recognized by central government, and other centres of curriculum development are being set up, with central government still tending to exert ultimate control and responsibility.	The inspectorate plays a key role in a traditional form of diffusion in a system where there is little decentralization; but a grass-roots movement to challenge central control is emerging.	There is considerable decentralization to teachers in schools through Teachers' Centres and other linking agencies. But there is also some myth-making about the degree of autonomy exercised by the school principal and the classroom teacher.

funded by SVO, the official educational research agency in the Netherlands.)

However, some major enterprises with a somewhat more theoretical and less pragmatic approach owe their support to university institutes of education. Others, more orientated towards the market, are wholly financed by major educational publishers such as Wolters-Noordhoff.

The growing Netherlands interest in heuristic curriculum development is reflected in a special concern with initial and in-service teacher education and in the sustained national debate which arose from the proposals put forward (in 1971) by the Commission on the Organization of Curriculum Development for a more coordinated pattern of management. But the prospect of any form of national agency (inevitably calling for additional resources) must depend on the restoration of the cutbacks in the national educational budget, which had in the past accounted for the highest proportion of GNP of any country in Western Europe.

A summary review

Using the analysis set out in this chapter, the Open University's course team for its course on Curriculum Design and Development has drawn up a summary in tabular form of the main characteristics of curriculum development in the three groups of countries we have distinguished.[8] The table brings together in a succinct and useful way the various points we have made, and we reproduce it on pages 32 and 33.

3 Patterns of control

Legal and administrative controls

For England and Wales the 1944 Education Act gave the Secretary of State a residual responsibility with a strictly limited discretion to carry it out. Its first clause confirmed that the education service was the responsibility of the Secretary of State (formerly Minister) and put the locally elected education authorities through whom he must work 'under his control and direction'. Under Section 68, he was vested with what seem at first sight to be sweeping powers. But these are more apparent than real – the House of Lords' judgement in the Tameside case (1976) showed how narrowly the courts were prepared to interpret them – and the sanctions supporting them are too severe, cumbersome and uncertain for frequent exercise.[1]

Responsibility for the curriculum – a term the Act used in its narrow sense – was vested in the local education authorities, and in the governors and managers of voluntary schools.[2] In practice, however, decisions about the curriculum are taken by teaching staff at the level of the individual school. Only an incident of exceptional local interest or sensitivity will prompt a governing or managing body to take any form of action on matters which are normally regarded as wholly within the professional discretion of the head and his staff.[3]

The strength and weakness of a public curriculum which is shrouded in mystery and changed by stealth has been most obvious in relation to the English primary school. On the one hand it could be said that changes which many people would regard as for the better would not have come about in the way they did had not the professionals enjoyed the freedom to put their own judgement above that of an apathetic or simply conservative community. On the other hand, critics would say that these changes merely show that any 'rational' and 'collective' idea of what society expects children to learn and do during the early years has disintegrated. A criticism of many primary schools is that they allow individual children to assemble their own curricula without making sure that they add up to a balanced primary schooling. The teaching (or lack of it) of reading is an example of how both school practices and individual teachers' values vary. Can a 'public' curriculum exist in the welter of variations?

A more balanced view suggests that a school which neglects the basic tool subjects is an exception to the great majority which still confidently recognize the primacy of reading, writing and number, while also giving prominence to a range of expressive subjects and practical activities. But, even so, recent attempts to develop agreed standards for basic subjects clearly flow from dissatisfaction with the vagueness which has surrounded the primary curriculum and recognition of the need to bring discussion of it back into the public arena.

Examinations

The secondary curriculum has one distinctive control in the shape of the system of external and externally moderated examinations – the General Certificate of Education Examination at Ordinary and Advanced Levels, and the Certificate of Secondary Education Examinations in their various modes. The way public oversight of the examination system has evolved shows a good deal about curriculum control in England and Wales.

The actual examinations are administered by autonomous examining bodies (eight concerned with GCE, fourteen with CSE). These are not subject to the direction of the Department of Education, but the Secretary of State is assumed to have residual authority for the system. He or she issues regulations for the CSE boards; GCE certificates are signed by a DES official. But since the end of the First World War the Secretary of State has relied on advice from an intermediary body and, in the English context, this soon means that some measure of control tacitly slips into the hands of that body until or unless some critical issue arises.

The Secondary Schools Examination Council (1917–63)

Until 1963 the advisory body on examination policy was the Secondary Schools Examination Council, set up originally to preside over the School Certificate Examination created in 1917. This was an unassertive body dominated by the representatives of the university examining boards. When the School and Higher School Certificates were replaced after the Second World War by GCE O and A Levels the then Minister, Miss Ellen Wilkinson, envisaged a more positive instrument to assist her in her 'full responsibility . . . for the direction of policy and general arrangements in regard to school examinations'.[4] In the event the Ministry of Education did not maintain an actively interventionist role. The reconstituted Council was dominated by teachers and local education authorities, with HM Inspectors of Schools playing the leading role in the secretariat.

It was the SSEC's duty to approve all the new GCE syllabuses at Ordinary and Advanced Level, and subject panels were set up for this purpose. It directed its attention largely to national standards, especially in ensuring equity between one set of examinees and another. Certainly it recognized the impact of syllabus changes on teaching practice; but when it intervened on the content of the subject curriculum itself and the effect of particular examination changes on, say, the teaching of a modern language or the approach to English grammar, it was to reflect the view of the educational establishment (especially the subject specialists in the Inspectorate) rather than to exercise any developmental function. It had neither the resources nor the inclination to speculate seriously on what the curriculum ought to be or how it could be changed for the better. The assumption was firmly made that the examination should follow the curriculum, not lead it. And, by its very nature, the SSEC was unwieldy, remote from classroom activities and, with the exception of the ever-diligent HMIs, composed of men whose other, more arduous appointments pre-empted their attentions and who had long since been removed from any intimate connection either with boys and girls or with scholarship. The SSEC, of course, was also concerned only with secondary schools, and, essentially, with the curriculum of some 25 per cent of those over the age of fourteen.

It was frequently at loggerheads with the examining boards. In a racy account of the examination system written in 1969,[5] George Bruce, then Secretary of the University of London Entrance and School Examination Council, attacked the post-1947 Secondary Schools Examination Council for its interfering role, and its failure to give the representatives of examination boards an influential part in its activities:

No reason has even been publicly stated; but the determination to keep them out persisted throughout the life of the reconstituted SSEC, in spite of every pointer towards the need for a full partnership between these two major interests in secondary school education. Possibly the heart of the matter is the view that the rules should be drawn up by amateurs and professionals should play the game. What has been singularly unfortunate has been that the amateurs have neither played the game nor seen it played, and they do not know what it is reasonable to expect.

In Bruce's context, the professionals are the professional examiners, meaning the army of moderators, chief examiners, assistant chief examiners and assistant examiners, who work with tireless energy to a merciless routine. How they set the draft papers, criticize the various drafts among themselves, recruit the examiners (with remarkably little turnover from year to year), train and supervise the assistant examiners and compare and adjust the marks to discount differences in marking severity, is a tribute to the care and professionalism which they have built up over many years. Fairness between one candidate and another, and between one generation and the next, is the paramount consideration. But in wielding its powerful influence the professional machine is impelled less by partisan views on what should, or should not, be done to the school curriculum than by the pressures and priorities of the examining process. The nature and the formidable strength of this professionalism must be held in mind in any consideration of who controls the examination and, through the examination, the public curriculum.

Within fifteen years of the reform which introduced the General Certificate of Education, the system was once more under strain. In the 1950s and early 1960s many pupils outside the grammar schools, in secondary modern, technical and, later, comprehensive schools, began to sit the GCE examination. Attempts to stem the growth of O Level in the modern schools failed. Heads and their staff refused to confine their students within a preconceived and limited set of expectations. In a short space of time, the success of the non-grammar schools came to be measured in terms of their ability successfully to offer O Level courses.[6]

Other examinations joined the O Level explosion, in particular those of the technical examining bodies, the Royal Society of Arts and the College of Preceptors. As examinations proliferated, costs rose, efforts were fragmented and doubts grew about the currency of the new qualifications. Neither the teaching profession nor the Ministry of Education had any control over the numerous examinations offered by many different bodies: anarchy reigned.

In 1911 a similar situation had caused the Board of Education to set up first an inquiry and then the School and Higher School Certificates; in 1955 Circular 289 of the Ministry not only rejected the demand for an examination for the modern schools but advised those schools not to seek prestige by pushing their pupils into O Levels. But still the numbers grew – both of non-grammar school pupils who stayed beyond the minimum school-leaving age and of examinations being taken in the fourth and fifth years of the secondary school.

In 1958 the Secondary Schools Examination Council was given the necessary encouragement to set up a small committee, chaired by Robert Beloe, Chief Education Officer for Surrey, to look at 'Secondary School Examinations other than the GCE'. When it reported in 1960 the committee recommended the introduction of a new examination to be known as the Certificate of Secondary Education, intended to scotch the growth of external examinations at the fourth-year stage. CSE was not to be taken before the fifth year – i.e. it was aimed at those staying on beyond the age of fifteen. Like GCE it was to be a single-subject examination, but catering mainly for the middle 40 per cent of the ability range. It was to be a national examination with a national body (in Beloe's view, a standing committee of the SSEC) to oversee national standards. But there was to be much more intimate teacher participation than for GCE and to this end there were to be more regional examining boards. Beloe envisaged twenty of them; in the event there were fourteen.

The Beloe proposals were developed and elaborated by the SSEC in the Council's fourth and fifth reports, and endorsed by the Minister in Circular 9/63. Three modes of examination were established:[7]

Mode 1
An external examination on syllabuses provided by the regional subject panels.

Mode 2
An external examination on syllabuses provided by a school or group of schools and approved by the regional subject panels.

Mode 3
Examinations set and marked internally in a school or group of schools, but moderated by the region.

The impending arrival of a new, more explicitly teacher-controlled examination coincided with the growing belief inside the Ministry of Education that some means had to be found to link consideration of the curriculum and consideration of examinations. There was, of course, nothing new in this perception. The Norwood Committee's terms of reference in 1941 had required it 'to consider suggested changes in the secondary school curriculum and the question of school examinations in relation thereto'.

The Schools Council (1964 onwards)

The new examination required development studies and the SSEC was clearly not the body to tackle them. The then Minister, Sir David Eccles, and others favoured the much bigger ministerial involvement in the curriculum entailed by a Curriculum Study Group within the Ministry of Education itself. Local authorities and the teachers' unions, however, responded to the Group's establishment with hostility and suspicion, and attempts to breathe life into it were frustrated by an alliance between Sir William (later Lord) Alexander, Secretary of the Association of Education Committees, and Sir Ronald Gould, General Secretary of the National Union of Teachers. Instead the interests of the Ministry, the l.e.a.s, the teachers' unions and other educationists were joined in a new body, the Schools Council. The assistant secretary in the Ministry of Education who had been in charge of the Curriculum Study Group, Derek Morrell, a man of great intellectual force, moved across to become one of the first joint secretaries of the new-found Council, as did his HMI counterpart, Robert Morris.

To this body was entrusted responsibility both for curriculum development and for the oversight of examinations (as successor to the SSEC). The Council took over from the Nuffield Foundation a series of curriculum development projects loosely based on the American research and development model, and began to invent others of its own. The new CSE exams were the first priority of its other role: the Council had to give reality to a concept of examining which left the maximum freedom to individual schools and teachers, while still achieving a necessary minimum of attention to national standards and comparability.

The Council incorporated the view that effective curriculum development in secondary schools depends on being able to reform the examination and examination syllabus alongside the subject curriculum, and that in principle the examination should follow the curriculum, not vice versa. Rhetoric has therefore all along insisted that the developmental side of the Council's work should dominate. But it is also a requirement that public examinations should be nationally fair, and this may inhibit more speculative kinds of innovation. The object of uniting responsibility for advice on both curriculum and examination is to hold a balance between these potentially conflicting interests and in theory the Schools Council should have been in a better position to do so than the old SSEC.

In fact the authority of the Council as successor to the SSEC has not yet been tested by any confrontation between a development project and an examination board, because the same people sit on interlocking committees and speak with different voices according to which mask they wear. There has been no significant shift of power to the Schools Council from the O and A Level boards, and the method of resolving difficulties remains the same – compromises are reached by give and take. Where new curricula suggest the need for new examinations, negotiations take place between the developers and the examining board or boards, and the pilot projects are set in motion. Some Schools Council development projects (notably the Modern Languages one) have felt their innovative imagination to have suffered from the curbs of examination exigencies, but for the most part the arrangement has worked smoothly. It may be noted, too, that before the Schools Council was invented the Nuffield Foundation had no difficulty in negotiating the various Nuffield science projects with the examining boards.

But in terms of the internal politics of the education system, a major change was taking place. The Department of Education and Science was ceding to a body controlled by the main teachers' union,[8] functions and responsibilities formerly carried out by a committee which had worked extremely closely with the Ministry and the Board of Education before it. Yet there had been no changes in law or in administrative philosophy to make the DES give up power over examinations.

The technique of supervising examinations also had to change. The old SSEC had required examining boards to submit all new

O and A Level syllabuses for approval, and had subjected these to close vetting. But the CSE examination defied any such close supervision. Not only were there nearly twice as many CSE boards as GCE boards, but the existence of three different modes hugely increased the number of syllabuses (one CSE board might approve more than 1000 different papers in a single subject). Had the Schools Council ever tried to monitor the CSE as its predecessor had monitored GCE, the flood of material would have submerged it. And, of course, because it gave the CSE boards their freedom, it had also to do the same for the GCE boards at O Level. (The Council still receives all new O Level syllabuses 'for comment' but no longer for approval; though new or substantially revised A Level syllabuses still require approval.)

So the expansion of secondary education from élite to mass proportions strained the traditional mechanism for the central control of the public curriculum. One issue facing the Schools Council was the pattern of examinations which should meet the needs of sixth-formers. The framework of the sixth form is important to the curricular shape of the educational system. But as sixth-form pupils grew in diversity progress towards a new framework was painfully slow. The idea of a five-subject sixth form was supported only by a frail and ambiguous consensus, and so needed a long time to acquire that sense of inevitability which can provide a substitute for enthusiasm.

What was lacking was any real commitment to a developmental approach. Here was a national curriculum development body engaged in major curriculum change, but the methods it used were largely the traditional ones of *a priori* reasoning, taking evidence, sounding opinion and seeking to mobilize agreement within the professional establishment. Exactly the same might be said of the attempt to merge GCE O Level and the CSE examination into a single system of examining at sixteen-plus.

The whole exercise was one of examination planning rather than of curriculum development. Individual examining boards prepared feasibility studies, the Schools Council assessed the results, made a judgement and put forward proposals to the Secretary of State. But the boards simply assumed that an appropriate curriculum would somehow emerge from within the system as a result of changes in the examination structure – in effect, they worked on the principle that if the cart is placed in position the horse will sooner or later put itself between the shafts. This exercise may fairly be said to represent a major retreat from the notion that the examinations should be subordinate to the curriculum. No doubt the Schools Council would in due course get round to a consideration of the curricular consequences of any new examination, but only as an afterthought. And the curricular consequences are considerable if the examination syllabus is narrowed to make easier the inherently difficult task of examining so broad a range of attainment at sixteen. The questions raised for a curriculum development body demand to be tackled by developmental methods, but again the traditional way of settling complicated arguments by assertion instead of experiment was allowed to triumph.

Direct intervention of the Department of Education and Science (from 1976)

The Schools Council's general proposals in the summer of 1976 for a single system of examining at sixteen-plus opened a new chapter in the history of public control over examinations and hence over the curriculum. The DES, under successive Secretaries of State, had for some years been re-establishing its own direct interest in the curriculum. One way was by setting up an Assessment of Performance Unit inside the DES (1974), which only the naïve would have failed to connect with widespread popular anxiety about standards of achievement in the basic skills, articulated in (and stirred up by) the Black Papers. This recognized that the Secretary of State, as ultimate custodian of the public curriculum, required a means to monitor what went on in primary and secondary schools and concentrate resources where under-performance revealed special need. The DES had, too, treated Schools Council advice on examinations with evident reserve.

Before the Secretary of State replied in the autumn of 1976 to the Schools Council, a major speech at Ruskin College by James Callaghan, the Prime Minister, signalled a new approach to public policy on the curriculum, with much more active intervention by the DES and HM Inspectorate. He picked up the issues raised by critics of the education system, and indicated that it was time for people other than teachers and educational administrators to become involved in the discussion of standards, the curriculum, and the connection between school and work.

In the changed diplomatic climate between the Schools Council and the DES, the new Secretary of State, Mrs Shirley Williams, neither accepted nor rejected the Council's proposals for a sixteen-plus examination. Instead she took the task of reorganizing the examination system into her own hands, using the Council's officers for assistance but not their committee system of decision-making, and setting up a new steering group, chaired by a former civil servant. In effect the Secretary of State was reviving some of the original plans for the Curriculum Study Group. At the same time, she urged the Schools Council to come forward with proposals for its own reform, along lines which would reduce the influence of the teachers' unions and increase that of the Department and of interests outside the education system.

Through the Schools Council, l.e.a.s and teachers had attempted to stem the growth of DES involvement; their success was short-term, lasting little more than a decade. But the relationships through which power is shared in English education were as complex as ever, and any instrument devised to make collective decisions would have to recognize this and accept the inevitable compromises. The power of the teachers' unions had been unexpectedly increased to the point where it became politically unacceptable. Once it was recognized that what was at issue was something much broader than the cognitive content of the narrow subject curriculum, the conventional wisdom – part myth and part reality – about where responsibility should rest was certain to change. Transactions between central and local government, teachers, parents and pupils would need to be conducted within a new set of conventions when the Great Debate initiated by Mr Callaghan had run its course.

Scottish sidelights

It was noticeable that the search for new conventions generated occasional sidelong glances at Scotland, where the structure of the system is different and different policies govern the management and development of the curriculum. The Scottish Education Department is responsible to the Scottish Secretary of State for the general supervision of the Scottish system of education, with the exception of the eight Scottish universities: these, like English and Welsh universities, depend largely upon grants received through the University Grants Committee.

In 1976 96·4 per cent of Scottish school pupils went to schools (with only a very few exceptions coeducational) run by nine regional and three island authorities. Within the education authorities are education committees which administer the schools by means of a professional directorate; some responsibilities, but not related to curriculum, are given to school councils. In the service of the authorities, and varying in number and type of responsibility, are specialist advisers with oversight of such areas or subjects as primary or secondary education, music, modern languages or physical education. Most of these advisers are involved in curriculum development, as are many of Her Majesty's Inspectors. Scotland does not have local inspectors.

Scottish education authorities manage and provide all financial support for over 400 Roman Catholic schools; in the remaining authority schools religious observances are held and religious education provided. RE is not, as other subjects in the curriculum are, subject to the inspection or approval of HMIs.

In several respects Scottish education may be described as centralized or unified. The General Teaching Council for Scotland, set up in 1966, advises the Secretary of State for Scotland on standards of training for and entry to teaching in Scotland. A majority of Council members are elected teachers. All Scottish teachers in education authority schools must be registered with the Council, which has powers of discipline. School head teachers report to the Council on probationers' ability as teachers.

Scotland has one examination system, till 1965 administered by the SED but now the responsibility of the Scottish Certificate of Education Examination Board which conducts examinations at three levels – Ordinary Grade, Higher Grade and Certificate of Sixth Year Studies.

In 1965 the Secretary of State for Scotland set up the Consultative Committee on the Curriculum. Teachers from most levels and sectors of education are appointed to this Committee; the teachers' unions do not elect any of the members. The Secretary of the SED (a civil servant) has chaired the CCC, which has appointed working parties and committees to study and report on various aspects of the curriculum. Several central committees with permanent staff and accommodation are responsible to the CCC, among them being committees on English, modern languages, science and social subjects.

The vast majority of Scottish pupils who move on to university studies go to Scottish universities, where in 1976–7 they constituted about 74 per cent of the student population, 15 per cent coming from the rest of the UK and 11 per cent from overseas. Other post-school education available to Scottish students is in further education colleges (administered by the regional authorities), colleges of education, and central institutions (roughly equivalent to English polytechnics). The colleges of education and the central institutions are controlled by the SED.

The Scottish Technical Education Council (Scotec) and the Scottish Business Education Council (Scotbec) have in Scotland functions similar to those of TEC and BEC in England and Wales.

Until recently teacher training in Scotland has been markedly unified: training has been provided for both primary and secondary teachers in colleges of education, of which in 1977 Scotland had ten. Secondary teachers have normally attended a college of education for a year after taking a university degree or comparable qualification. The primary teacher has either done the same or has taken a three-year college diploma course. In recent years four-year B.Ed. degree courses have been introduced; these have been run jointly by colleges along with universities or with CNAA approval. Also, at Stirling University, where education is a subject studied at undergraduate level, teacher training may be combined with degree courses.

Not least through the Scottish Inspectorate there is a continuing awareness and influence from thought and action on curriculum development in England. For instance, Scotland attempted no equivalent to the Bullock Report *A Language for Life*, which has been influential in curriculum thinking in Scotland through the CCC's central committee on primary education and in other ways.

4 Agents of change

National objectives

Curriculum development can only take place within a framework of public education policy, however tenuously linked to this policy and to the public system of education the developer may be. How then are national objectives formulated? The method (or non-method) prevailing in England and Wales and the practice adopted by a centralized and self-consciously systematic European neighbour, Sweden, illustrate contrasting approaches.

Speaking to the Society of Education Officers in London in 1973, Mr Edward Heath, then Prime Minister, said:

We try as a society to indicate to the professionals the human values, the social attitudes, the cultural traditions, the range of skills we wish them to foster in the young people we entrust to their charge. Thereafter we leave it to their professional responsibility and expertise to decide how to translate our wishes into courses and syllabuses and methods of teaching and learning designed as far as possible to meet the needs of each individual.

The impression intended and conveyed by this polite rhetoric was that it was up to the education officers to get on with the job of running the schools and that as a politician Mr Heath would defend their right to exercise their professional autonomy in doing so. What he actually said, however, exposed the vacuum in English curriculum development: very little is done by our society, in any formal way, 'to indicate to the profession the human values, the social attitudes, the cultural traditions, the range of skills we wish them to foster in the young . . .'

The tidy picture presented by his scriptwriter as the orthodox rationale of the curriculum and its development in fact bore little resemblance to reality. Society has not in the past decided on the goals first, and then left it to the schools to work out the curriculum to attain them. Indeed the last formal opportunity Parliament has had to concentrate its collective mind on the major public goals of education and how they should be systematically pursued in schools and colleges was the deliberations which went into the Education Act of 1944. The Great Debate of 1977, and the Green Paper which followed it, represented the first serious attempt to change this.

It is unlikely that the politicians have been headed off from curricular questions by their own modesty or indolence or reluctance to build empires. Rather there is a belief that definitive statements about educational goals, by those empowered to speak for the community, must be either vague (and banal) or precise (and dangerously restrictive) – a belief paralleled by Harold Nicolson's entry in his diary for 22 January 1941: 'Winston refused to make a statement on war aims. The reason given in Cabinet is that precise aims would be compromising, whereas vague principles would disappoint.'[1] This pragmatic reluctance to trust in brief verbal formulations of issues of surpassing complexity has been joined to specific doubts about the feasibility of separating ends and means in education. (The Green Paper of 1977 tends to confirm the wisdom of this scepticism.)

It seems a safe guess that most of the influential people in English education over the past quarter of a century have believed that the larger national educational objectives and the procedures to carry them out are inextricably linked; in other words, the dichotomy which Mr Heath assumed is a false one. And if it is false – if there is no profound or useful way in which one set of people (the politicians) can reach conclusions about objectives, and pass these on to another subordinate group (the educators) to translate into school programmes – then the consequences of any practical attempt to take Mr Heath's doctrine seriously would be unsatisfactory in the extreme. Either everyone would soon tire of the whole process and wilt under the weight of empty generalization, or else the politicians and administrators would feel obliged to go beyond objectives to much more specific discussion of the procedures by which these objectives might be attained. Professional prerogatives would then be invaded by the politicians and their administrative aides, and the separation of functions would be swept away.

It may be argued that, in educational terms, a pluralism of method and interpretation intensifies the difficulty of defining goals precisely, and that diverse and possibly contradictory activities could and would be justified on the grounds that they were intended to yield the same end result. The larger the aim, the more difficult the evaluation and the harder it must be to pin precise educational consequences on particular educational practices.

This characteristically English response to talk about goals and objectives in education is not, however, the only possible response. To find a country where a serious attempt has been made to establish national educational goals and to offer these, ready-made, to the professional educators as the basis of curriculum planning, it is necessary to go no further than Sweden.

In the Western world Sweden has made some of the most conscientious efforts to ensure that what happens in school is consistent with the larger aims of society – a society, incidentally, whose homogeneous character is reflected in the dominance of the Social Democrats as the party of government from the early 1930s until the 1976 election. This strong political consensus carries with it a commitment to the democratic ideal, and to what has been called the 'democratic value promise' that 'privileges in any field that cannot be justified on rational grounds should not be allowed to continue'.[2]

An OECD document which states these ideals goes on to quote five general goals.

Objective 1
All Swedes of school age should enjoy equal right to public education, without regard to income, social origin, sex, or place of residence. And since all individuals are 'born equal' and are endowed with talents and personality potentials that differ but are in all cases capable of development:
   (a) the aim of the school system should be to meet the differentiated needs of various groups of students, and
   (b) no one branch of education should in itself be considered more worthy of esteem than any other, the entire school system constituting a coordinated whole.

Objective 2
The school should aim at safeguarding and strengthening the democratic system. It follows . . . that:
   . . . there should be a considerable common core of learning, particularly in the comprehensive, but also in the upper secondary school;
   . . . provision should be made for frequent group work and discussion to strengthen cooperation and tolerance among the pupils;
   . . . particular attention should be given to fostering an understanding of the functions of the Swedish and other social systems;
   . . . critical and independent thinking should be encouraged . . .

Objective 3
Educational policy should contribute to general economic development, e.g. by producing the required types and amounts of qualified

manpower. However, this goal is often subordinate to the first two . . .

Objective 4
The educational system should be made more flexible to fit the shifting talents, interests and plans of the pupils . . . as well as a continuously changing labour market. This . . . requires flexibility in administrative procedure and in planning ('rolling planning') as well as a continuous or 'rolling' reform throughout the educational system. Such flexibility is necessary in order to enable the system:
  . . . to change itself in response to the changing structure of demand . . . by individual members of the society as well as the equally dynamic requirements of the economy;
  . . . to provide sufficient breadth . . . to allow for changes in students' school careers . . . thus eliminating 'dead ends' in the system.

Objective 5
The educational system should make efficient use of limited human and real resources.

It requires a considerable effort of the imagination to see, in these paragraphs, objectives which represent the prior considerations on which subsequent development could be founded – still less to which it could be linked by rigorous deductive and analytical processes. It may be more illuminating to look at them as one striking reflection of the ideological context of the later 1960s, when the systems approach was in its heyday as an instrument of curriculum and educational planning. But in so far as objectives were written down at all, they were the subsequent rationalization of objectives already deemed to be implicit within the system – a justification for on-going activities rather than a fundamental attempt by the community (acting at an early stage of the development process) to determine educational goals *de noro*.

The various committees which prepared the curricular instructions sent out to schools by the Swedish National Board of Education, however, enabled large numbers of people drawn from many different sections of the community to express what they perceived to be the educational consequences of national social policy.

It is important also to recognize that these community representatives have not confined themselves to statements of general goals. They have been drawn (thus confirming orthodox English expectations) right into the detailed discussion of content and methods as well – and in so doing have tacitly acknowledged that it is only in terms of process that many of the more specific and functional objectives can be stated.

The use of advisory councils

In England and Wales lack of systematic provision for public discussion of educational ends and means has meant that responsibility for such matters has been absorbed into the private domain of the large body of teachers, administrators, academics and laymen who collectively form the educational establishment. This gives significance to the most public form of traditional curriculum development conducted at national level in England and Wales – the major commissions of inquiry,[3] including the Board of Education's Consultative Committee and its successors, the Central Advisory Councils. In the inter-war period two of the consultative committee's reports – *The Education of the Adolescent* in 1926 and the 1931 Report on *Primary Education* – can be seen as major contributions to curriculum development, as later were such documents as the Crowther, Newsom and Plowden Reports.

The full-scale inquiry technique requires more or less eminent men and women, most of them involved in one way or another with making the existing system work, to consider the current practice of the schools and the directions in which development should move. They ponder the evidence submitted by political and professional pressure groups, as well as that provided by surveys and impressionistic studies carried out on the committee's behalf – and increasingly use commissioned research, though always as a supplement to more traditional methods of finding out which way the professional and administrative wind is blowing, and speculating on which way it ought to blow in the future.

They present their reflections on this evidence in a report which is expected to include relevant sections on subjects within the curriculum as well as about the organized relationship of the different activities which make up the whole. Thus, the last quarter of the Hadow Report of 1926[4] is devoted to 'Suggestions on the teaching of the several subjects of the curriculum in modern schools and senior classes', making it clear that the report concerned the curriculum in its narrow sense, just as the major proposals for the reorganization of post-primary education concerned the wider curriculum. Important chapters of the Crowther Report of 1959[5] concerned the teaching provision for the sixteen- to eighteen-year-olds in schools, and the rationale the committee offered of the specialized English sixth-form education can be viewed as a piece of traditional curriculum development, if only because the justification which it provided exposed the weaknesses of much of the argument on which the conventional sixth-form programme was based.

The Plowden Report[6] was the most self-conscious attempt to look at the curriculum of the primary school since the Hadow study of 1931 and perhaps marked the peak of traditional curriculum development. It appeared in 1967, just as the new heuristic approach to curriculum development was coming to first fruition in England and Wales. It made extensive use of research studies and of the services of the Inspectorate for the collection of information – including the appraisal of individual schools and the teaching methods they used, on the basis of the subjective, though practised, judgement of individual observers. And it developed a clear and optimistic point of view which gave force to its recommendations.

Chapter 15 of the Plowden Report contained a series of passages which sought to weave into a reasonably coherent pattern the threads of modern primary education, threads which could be traced clearly to the same skein of material from which the consultative committee's Report of 1931 had come. The committee rejected any attempt at a comprehensive definition of the aims of primary education on the traditional English ground that this could only lead to meaningless platitudes, but wrote three famous paragraphs at the end of the chapter which summed up what they thought good primary schools were about.

A school is not merely a teaching shop, it must transmit values and attitudes. It is a community in which children learn to live first and foremost as children and not as future adults. In family life children learn to live with people of all ages. The school sets out deliberately to devise the right environment for children, to allow them to be themselves and to develop in the way and at the pace appropriate to them. It tries to equalise opportunities and to compensate for handicaps. It lays special stress on individual discovery, on first-hand experience and on opportunities for creative work. It insists that knowledge does not fall into neatly separate compartments and that work and play are not opposite but complementary. A child brought up on such an atmosphere at all stages of his education has some hope of becoming a balanced and mature adult and of being able to live in, to contribute to, and to look critically at the society of which he forms a part. Not all primary schools correspond to this picture, but it does represent a general and quickening trend.

Some people, while conceding that children are happier under the modern regime and perhaps more versatile, question whether they are being fitted to grapple with the world which they will enter when they leave school. This view is worth examining because it is quite widely held, but we think it rests on a misconception. It isolates the long-term objective, that of living in and serving society, and regards education as being at all stages recognisably and specifically a preparation for this. It fails to understand that the best preparation for being a happy and useful man or woman is to live fully as a child. Finally, it assumes, quite wrongly, that the older virtues, as they are usually called, of neatness, accuracy, care and perseverance, and the sheer knowledge which is an essential of being educated, will decline: these are genuine virtues and an education which does not foster them is faulty.

Society is right to expect that importance will be attached to these virtues in all schools. Children need them and need knowledge, if they are to gain satisfaction from their education. What we repudiate is the view that they were automatically fostered by the old kind of elementary education. Patently they were not, for enormous numbers of the products of that education do not possess them. Still more we repudiate the fear that the modern primary approach leads to their neglect. On the contrary it can, and, when properly understood, does lay a much firmer foundation for their development and it is more in the interests of the children. But those interests are complex. Children need to be themselves, to live with other children and with grown-ups, to learn from their environment, to enjoy the present, to get ready for the future, to create and to love, to learn to face adversity, to behave responsibly, in a word, to be human beings. Decisions about the influences and situations that ought to be contrived to these ends must be left to individual schools, teachers and parents. What must be ensured is that the decisions taken in schools spring from the best available knowledge and are not simply dictated by habit or convention.

These paragraphs (505–7) have been dissected with much severity by Professor Richard Peters and others, who complain about the mixture of rhetoric and ideology which they present. But if they never came to grips with the objectives of primary school education in a manner rigorous enough to satisfy the philosophers, the Plowden committee gave their backing to one particular tendency in primary education: that combination of informal methods which cannot be defined or described with any precision but goes – abroad, if not at home – by the name of open education or 'the British primary school'.

If the report of an advisory council or consultative committee is the most obvious product of its deliberation, it is by no means the only one. Before specific recommendations which may lead to government actions are produced, the long-drawn-out process of consultation and argument has its own impact. One hundred and thirteen organizations and one hundred and seventy-seven individuals submitted written papers to Plowden. Thirty organizations sent delegates to engage in oral discussion with the committee; sixty-seven individuals, as well as twenty-seven HMIs and ex-HMIs and twenty other officials of the Department of Education and Science, also gave evidence. Such an inquiry focuses attention wonderfully. Immediately pervasive effects are apparent in the educational press and in the topics of discussion at the educational conferences which reflect the dominant concerns of the profession from year to year.

The committee of inquiry approach, though usually weak on research, is strong on consultation and the collection of opinions within the system. While specific proposals may be made directly to the government, the local authorities and the teachers the final results seldom comprise the kind of recommendations which a Secretary of State can accept or reject *in toto*, unless by chance there are a few clear-cut issues. Dissemination depends on the capacity of large numbers of individual teachers and administrators to absorb and internalize changes of emphasis which together point the way towards modest, incremental change. Curricular recommendations in conventional subject terms are fed into the system of blurred responsibilities and shared assumptions – a system which produces both the limited autonomy of teachers and the network of constraints which impose a measure of orthodoxy on secondary education and, to a lesser extent, on primary education too.

The weakness of the major educational inquiry as the English use it is obvious enough. Only a narrow range of non-professional opinion is tapped and the great majority of the participants, being themselves pillars of the system, often seem intent on extending the educational imperium over questions of value – about which the community as well as the professionals might seem entitled, as Mr Heath observed, to have news.

During the late 1960s and early 1970s the committee of inquiry system came into increasing disfavour with the Department of Education and Science and the politicians who then headed it, for three reasons. First, it was held that large-scale reviews of aspects and sections of the education service invariably gave rise to expensive proposals for development; second, the traditional method of filling places on such committees from within the system usually led them to produce a set of recommendations for 'more of the same' rather than to undertake any more fundamental appraisal; and third, such committees usually took about three years to report, and held up policy-making in the meantime. Section 4 of the 1944 Education Act laid down that there should be two Central Advisory Councils, one for England and one for Wales; that the Secretary of State should appoint the members and the chairman, together with a secretary who is to be a member of the Department; that members should be drawn from both the public and independent systems of education; and that, while the Secretary of State should make appointments for set periods of time and regulate the arrangements for meetings, the Council could largely determine its own procedure. But the Act does not, it seems, actually oblige the Secretary of State to keep a Council in being at any time to carry out its statutory duty of offering advice; and indeed from 1968 – when the Welsh Central Advisory Council completed its inquiry into primary education – until the time of writing, the Department of Education has kept the Council in abeyance.

Admittedly, politicians have continued to use the committee technique (or, when in opposition, to promise inquiries, thus demonstrating their reforming zeal). In recent years there have been formal inquiries by departmental committees into, among other things, adult education, reading and the education of handicapped children. After the 1970 general election Mrs Margaret Thatcher attempted to initiate a new technique by setting up a smaller group of full- and part-time members, led by Lord James, to review the education of teachers. The hope was that skilled analysis would thus be produced more quickly, and the planning staff of the Department of Education and Science would be more closely involved. The committee did indeed report in less than a year, as compared with the three years or so which the traditional inquiry might have been expected to take, but the method suffered from the defects of its virtues. Its very speed foreclosed the process of educating those who submitted evidence, and its small membership reduced its value as a kind of jury for the establishment.

The influence of HM Inspectors

The central government agency to whom most responsibility for traditional curriculum development has fallen hitherto has been the Inspectorate – the men and women known as Her Majesty's Inspectors (HMIs) who serve as the professional advisers and the eyes and ears of the Education Department. Now less then 500 strong, they have always enjoyed a measure of professional autonomy, as their title implies: but they are in fact appointed by the Secretary of State rather than by the Crown, and it is well established that they may receive direct instructions from him as to their duties. The Senior Chief Inspector is ranked with the Deputy Secretaries within the hierachy of the Department.

The Inspectorate was first formed to oversee and evaluate the spending of public money by the teacher-training institutions and schools which received grants from the state, but an advisory function always existed alongside the judgemental. In recent years, as the formal inspection has become much less important, so the advisory role has taken pride of place.[7] The methods they have used have been those of traditional curriculum development.

The contribution of the Inspectorate to the major reports of the consultative committees and the advisory councils has already been mentioned. More directly, the Inspectorate has been responsible for a succession of handbooks and pamphlets on aspects of curriculum content and teaching method. Even while the rigid policies of Morant were imposing a traditional grammar-school pattern upon the new county secondary schools during the first decade of the present century, the HMIs' first *Handbook of Suggestions for the Consideration of Teachers and Others Concerned in the Work of Public Elementary Schools* (1905) demonstrated the Inspectors' willingness to replace direct prescription by exhortation and advice. This, and the subsequent revised versions published in 1909, 1918, 1926 and 1937 put down on paper the nearest thing which existed to the official view, the view that a member of the Inspectorate would take with him when he visited schools, the view which teachers would reflect back to him if they were disposed to enjoy his approbation.

From the start a view of the teacher's role – a somewhat elevated view, much influenced, maybe, by the high ideals transmitted by Dr Arnold and his disciples to the public school men who were deliberately recruited to run the Inspectorate during these formative years – was expressed in the prefatory memorandum to the first *Handbook*: 'the only uniformity of practice that the Board of Education desires to see in the teaching of Public Elementary Schools is that each teacher shall think for himself and work out for himself such methods of teaching as may use his powers to the best advantage and be suited to the needs and conditions of the school.'

The facts of the Code and the practice of the elementary schools went a long way to belie this grand statement of intent, but the assumptions behind it explain a great deal about the subsequent evolution of the Inspectorate and the direction which curriculum development took in the primary school. In 1926 the curriculum clauses of the Elementary Code were discarded and the *Handbook of Suggestions* became the main vehicle by which the public curriculum of the elementary school was conveyed.

The pamphlets prepared by members of the Inspectorate and widely distributed to schools, education authorities and teacher training institutions also played their part in development. Many of these have been devoted to the teaching of particular subjects: for example, language (*Some suggestions for Teachers of English*, 1954), *Music in Schools* (1956), *Towards World History* (1967). Again, the idea has been to combine the wisdom of experience with sound *a priori* reasoning to produce a balanced view of current developments in a subject or area of study and draw attention to those which seem the most promising. The wisdom and reasoning brought to bear on a given topic are not peddled as a prescription, but offered as advice – and teachers and publishers make such use of it as they think fit.

The Inspectorate's role is central to the development of a more activist Department of Education and Science, and even before the Prime Minister's intervention the Senior Chief Inspector had set in hand changes aimed at increasing the effectiveness of the Inspectorate. A series of studies of different aspects of the primary and secondary examination curriculum had been put in hand, leading to what can be seen as the resumption of the policy of publishing critical pamphlets. (For example, the review of *Modern Languages in Comprehensive Schools* published by HMSO, at the time of the regional conferences held in the winter of 1976–7, helped to focus attention on controversial issues such as mixed ability teaching.)

It is important to distinguish between the curriculum development function of the Inspectorate in primary and secondary schools – where the advisory role has overtaken regulating duties – from those of the Further Education Inspectorate. The latter retained a direct responsibility for the approval of courses until the mid-1970s. Their work married important curricular discretion with administrative obligations, and so produced in the colleges of further education a degree of control over the curriculum unlike any exercised by the central government over primary and secondary education. Although their object was to prevent the growth of uneconomic courses and to promote the efficient use of resources, they could not pursue this object without impinging on the curriculum.

The role of local authorities

Like the Department of Education and Science, each local education authority is constantly engaged in policy-making and administration, with a consequent impact upon the curriculum. For example, the l.e.a. is involved with the central government in establishing priorities for school building. It controls the capitation allowances which are available for books, stationery and materials, and the supply or denial of extra funds to finance extra teaching materials for certain kinds of subject-based curriculum development. Ideas like 'positive discrimination' increase the interventionist role of the l.e.a., and hence the l.e.a.'s potential influence in curriculum development.

For much of this century the semi-autonomy allowed to education committees by the county and county borough councils of which they were subsidiary institutions has been reinforced by the financial mechanisms chosen by the central government. Thus the personality and educational philosophy of individual Chief Education Officers has had a powerful effect on traditional curriculum development. Men such as Sir Alec Clegg (West Riding of Yorkshire, 1947–74), Stewart C. Mason (Leicestershire, 1947–71) and A. R. Chorlton (Oxfordshire, 1945–70) were able to initiate development in the directions of their choice. By the same token, other CEOs could move in other directions, or decide to mark time where they were.

But the ending (in 1958) of percentage grants as the means of providing Exchequer support for education spending by local authorities – that is, the payment by the state of a fixed proportion of all approved expenditure by authorities – initiated the move to bring education more fully into line with other local government services. This move culminated with the reorganization of local government areas and functions in the Local Government Act of 1972, and the application of the corporate management techniques associated with it. Corporate management has not yet had time to be put fully to the test, but it must be expected to rely less on individual dynamism and to bring to the fore a different, less charismatic leadership. In theory, too, it must be expected to be more eager to evaluate the claims of the educators.

Many a Chief Education Officer has been able to influence appointments so as to build up a cadre of staff in whom he has confidence – placing his chosen candidates in key posts in the schools and the advisory services. As local authority inspectors, organizers and advisers – the terms vary more often than the functions – share with the HMIs the agency for promoting traditional development at local level, this influence is highly important. Clearly, it has its dangers. But English and Welsh l.e.a.s, in practice, have not simply steered people into jobs to promote a single point of view or direction of innovation. Most reformist aims have lacked careful definition, and therefore a valued characteristic of the traditional development process has been to preserve a variety of points of view – to go, if such an ideal is possible, for something as elusive as 'quality' at the expense of unanimity, and to make a virtue of the ensuing pluralism.

This pluralism has also been reinforced from another direction. As we have noted, the philosophy behind the open primary school movement has served to emphasize the professional autonomy and responsibility of the individual teacher. The leading exponents of this distinctively English curriculum development have insisted that, if head teachers were to be encouraged to give professional discretion to their assistant teachers, so, too, the Chief Education Officers and their advisory staff must respect the independent professional judgement of the heads. The development of modern primary school education in, say, Leicestershire has owed a great deal to the appointment of certain key individuals – specialist advisers with new ideas to introduce and new confidence to offer; heads who not only demonstrated by their own efforts how schools could be changed but also trained deputies who, in their turn, moved on elsewhere, to reproduce and embellish the model on which they had gained their own experience.

In-service training, where it has been most successful and highly valued (as for example in the old West Riding of Yorkshire before local government reorganization), has drawn upon these outstanding individuals to develop techniques of adult education – and skills in running conferences – which enable them to transmit experience as well as knowledge to fellow-professionals.

Teaching materials

Reference has been made in the last chapter to the influence of public examinations upon the curriculum. The examination requirements sum up in a series of outline syllabuses the examiners' interpretations of contemporary expectations and thus provide guidelines within which the writers of textbooks can work. Within these guidelines, traditional development has relied upon the individual enterprise of writers and publishers to produce books or series of books and offer them to the teachers on their merits. 'Merit' has been assumed to be ascribed by the teachers through their individual choices.

Traditional curriculum development therefore relies, perhaps optimistically, on the idea of a 'market' for innovation and market mechanisms for the transmission of the fruits of curriculum development. The route runs from the innovative author, the popular interpreter of a new line of educational thinking, via commercial publishers to the schools which control the limited funds available, and which in turn decide whether or not to reward him for his efforts.[8] This market process has emphasized the individualistic nature of development, but it has also made for uniformity. The fashions of professional taste and the demands of the examination system have led in some major subjects to the virtual domination of the classrooms by a few popular texts.[9]

From traditional to heuristic

Much traditional curriculum development has gone unrecognized as such, because it falls outside the limits of the narrowly conceived definition of 'the curriculum'. A more self-conscious recognition of the many forms of professional activity which belong under the curriculum development umbrella is necessary before discussion can be fined down to meet the limiting criteria suggested in Chapter 1.

A wider perception of the nature of curriculum change had already begun to develop in England before the much publicized advent of new methods in North America in the late 1950s. The twin exigencies of the rapidly rising birth rate and the virtual moratorium on school building during and just after the war meant that a large school building programme was needed in a hurry and costs had to be balanced against the educational functions of the new schools. To develop controlling techniques the Architects and Buildings Branch within the Ministry of Education formed a development group, drawing on ideas worked out in Hertfordshire and elsewhere which brought together administrators, architects and educators into a single team. While the architects sought to interpret effectively the requirements of those who would have to work in the buildings they planned, the designs produced from this dialectic not merely reflected the practices of the school: they also influenced them. One obvious example can be found in the movement towards open-plan design for primary schools and the pull–push relationship which this has generated between the economics of school building and the advancement of primary school pedagogy. In Winston Churchill's words, 'we shape our buildings and afterwards our buildings shape us'.

This is not the place to offer a snap evaluation of the lasting effect of the Ministry's development group, or to trace in detail the process by which, as time went on, economic considerations displaced educational ideals to a point at which, in the early 1970s, inflation effectively undermined the administrative edifice so laboriously created over the previous decade and more. It is enough to point to those consequences of the multi-disciplinary approach to school building which forced curricular issues out into the open. If school design shapes the activities which take place within the school, it shapes the curriculum; if it shapes the curriculum, should not this be subject to systematic development techniques, as other aspects of school design and technology might be? The architects' development group became, in the event, a bridge between traditional curriculum development and the heuristic approach. The Curriculum Study Group of the early 1960s was consciously modelled on that which had transformed the approach to school building. For various reasons, the Schools Council emerged as the residuary legatee of the Ministry's Curriculum Study Group at the very moment in time when the heuristic curriculum development movement gathered momentum.

It was the North American example which helped to generate that momentum. The spectacular success of Russian space technology in launching the first sputnik in 1957 dramatized the issue of technical achievement in a form which opened up the flow of public funds for development. But already the progressive 'life adjustment' education movement in the United States was in retreat and exponents of 'discipline-centred' education, many of them leading university scientists, had begun to mount their challenge to the secondary school curriculum. With a new urgency went a new strategy which drew heavily on the technologies which had been developed in the defence and aerospace industries. The essence of the approach was its rational, problem-solving basis. It assumed that clear-headed scrutiny of present practice would reveal what was good and what was bad. There was the hope that a recognizably 'best' way of organizing learning could be discovered and then applied. It was assumed that national shortcomings in scientific achievement could be traced to specific shortcomings in the school curriculum. Likewise, it was assumed that the curriculum could be remodelled to remedy perceived weaknesses by drawing on the best-available expertise inside the schools – and, even more, outside them.

The optimism of the North American new-style curriculum developers was infectious. By the early 1960s the science curricula in secondary schools were also being questioned on this side of the Atlantic. The moving spirits in England and Wales were the Science Masters' Association and the Association of Women Science Teachers (later joined to form one of the strongest of the subject teachers' groups, the Association for Science Education). Soon after the launching of the American Physical Science Study Committee (PSSC) programme financed by the National Science Foundation under the leadership of Professor Jerrold Zacharias, the associations mounted a series of conferences from which they produced new O Level science examination syllabuses for discussion. Their work engaged the interest of scientists in industry, of the Royal Society, and of the Advisory Council on Scientific Policy, whose chairman, Lord Todd, happened also to be a trustee of the Nuffield Foundation. A major outcome was the science curriculum programme sponsored in 1962 by the Nuffield Foundation. Instead of just promoting new O Level syllabuses and thus seeking by the traditional method to change practice, the Nuffield trustees decided that a full-scale development project should be launched. This would necessarily involve revised O Level examinations, but the important change of emphasis was that the new examination would follow a reappraisal of the curriculum, not precede it.

Significantly, the Nuffield approach, unlike the North American example, recognized that an English curriculum project needed to draw heavily on the expertise of the best practising teachers. University specialists might help in particular ways, but not, as in the United States, as the presiding geniuses and moving spirits. The Nuffield Foundation went on to sponsor a number of other projects on similar lines (in mathematics, modern languages and classics) and continued to play an active part in the school curriculum till the late 1960s. In due course, however, the Schools Council emerged as the major institution engaged in heuristic forms of development.

The Council's predominant concern (like that of the Nuffield Foundation) with subject-based development had certain direct consequences. First, because in-service training (an important element in traditional curriculum development) was outside the Council's remit, no fully satisfactory links between development and this essential part of the dissemination process have yet been made. The finance of in-service training is the responsibility of the DES on the one hand and the local authorities on the other. A sharp dichotomy between the traditional and heuristic forms of curriculum development was ensured, and thus the implication of the wider definition of the curriculum has been lost.

Secondly, a belated attempt to take account of system-wide considerations exposed the limitations of subject-based development. The Schools Council had no over-arching theory of the whole curriculum – indeed there is none in the context of the English education system of the 1960s and 1970s. Nor will it emerge from the pursuit of innovation in one separate subject area after another. When the Council has sought to complement this piecemeal approach by setting up projects on 'the curriculum as a whole' the resort has been not to heuristic developmental methods, but to the old familiar working party or discussion group, with predictably marshmallow results.

5 Subject-based development

There were good reasons why curriculum development agencies initially preferred subject-based projects. In the first place, it is much easier to organize a development project which has a clear and limited set of aims. System-based development – that is, a change in curricular process designed to affect the system as a whole, or some sub-system within it – has to grapple with general goals, and to tackle the business of translating them into the specifics of classroom practice across the whole range of curriculum subjects (and often across a wide range of age and ability as well). It may have to cope at the same time with rearrangements in the structure and organization of schools. Subject-based developers, on the other hand, can set themselves a less daunting task: they may challenge the established traditions of teaching a particular subject, but seldom go further than this. They do not usually demand a radical change in educational policy, and they rarely make big demands upon the way schools as a whole are run.

In the second place, subject-based developments promise more immediate and tangible, if less ambitious, results. Although in practice it may take a long time – up to a decade at least – for even a successful curriculum project to have any major effect on the educational system, the timespan of the actual development process can be limited to three or four years. A sponsoring agency can more easily persuade itself that it is getting visible value for its money; and, of course, the costs of the exercise are relatively more modest and easier to control than they are for a system-based programme.

Historically, too, subject-based development has often found it easier to enlist support because of its appeal to sectional interest groups, many of which are closely knit and well organized. The 'science lobby' in the USA was a powerful influence behind such programmes as the Physical Science Study Committee's project for high school physics, while in England and Wales, teacher interest groups, such as the Association for Science Education, the Mathematical Association, the Modern Languages Association and the Joint Association of Classics Teachers, threw their weight behind curriculum reform programmes in their respective subject areas. (It can be remarked, incidentally, that subject-based curriculum programmes seem to follow a common sequence in country after country: in Germany, in the Netherlands and in Sweden, as in the USA and the UK, initial projects in science and mathematics have been followed after an interval by modern language programmes and only later by projects in less highly structured subjects such as social studies.)

In contrast, an ambitious system-based reform programme which challenges fundamental educational norms is politically more controversial. It is also ideologically less acceptable in a decentralized educational system, and those countries with a decentralized approach show an historical preference for subject-based development. Such a preference harmonizes with the process of piecemeal social engineering, espoused by Karl Popper, in its refusal to take on too much at once in the way of utopian reform, and in its preference for a gradualist approach in which subsequent efforts can profit from previous experience.

The process of learning from past mistakes can be clearly seen in the history of subject-based projects. Three basic approaches can be distinguished, termed by Havelock[1] the Research, Development and Diffusion (RD and D) model, the Social-interaction model and the Problem-solving model, each of which seems to have evolved as a reaction to the perceived limitations of its predecessor.

The RD and D model

The reasoning behind the RD and D approach is intuitively attractive. In simplified terms, it first asks what are the underlying aims of teaching that subject with whose development it is concerned. Next it considers what is known about the best methods of achieving those aims. Finally, it applies those methods to the presentation of the required subject content. Appropriate teaching materials can then be devised, tried out, revised in the light of the trials and made generally available. The resulting product, based on agreed aims, and perfected by field trials, must be virtually certain to meet classroom needs.

The apparent logic of such a strategy has convinced most of the agencies responsible for initiating programmes of subject-based development in countries as diverse as Germany, Sweden, the UK and the USA. But subsequent experience shows that it does not always work as neatly in practice as it should in theory. To discover why, it may be useful to look more closely at each of the successive stages.

To start with, it is by no means easy to identify aims, or even to agree on the function in the curriculum of any given subject. Many chemistry teachers, for example, would disagree about whether knowing the properties of the elements is more important than knowing how to determine the composition of an unidentified substance. Modern language teachers may disagree about whether their main aim should be to develop skills of oral communication, or to generate an appreciation of the classical literature, or to help pupils understand the workings of a different society from their own. These are value positions, not matters of fact: research findings can only help in a crude, head-counting way ('60 per cent of biology teachers believe . . .').

Moreover, the more specific the statement of curricular aims the more controversial it is likely to be. An extreme insistence on precisely defined behavioural objectives ('at the end of the course, a pupil will be able to (a) enumerate the causes of the Peninsular War . . .') in any case reduces the curriculum to a series of atomistic accomplishments which fail to add up to an organic and coherent whole. Yet a definition of aims which is general enough to be widely acceptable will give little practical guidance to anyone struggling to develop a new curriculum. To find a middle way between being comprehensive and vacuous and being specific and stultifying is far from easy.

Having decided on aims, the RD and D model then calls upon research to reveal the best teaching method. But the brute fact is that very little is known about how people learn. Research on human learning, straitjacketed by the laboratory techniques of classical physics, has tended to concentrate largely on the acquisition of relatively simple practical skills, many of them divorced from normal experience. Much of the useful information about the best ways to help pupils acquire particular types of intellectual accomplishment is intuitive or anecdotal rather than scientific and systematic.

For example, the 'discovery'[2] approach of the American Physical Science Study Committee's programme and the Nuffield O Level Physics Project seems inherently reasonable. Both took the view that it was more important for pupils to learn the concepts and methods of physics – to get inside the skin of physicists, so to speak – than to master lists of its factual contents: and therefore they should, wherever possible, be made to work out for themselves solutions to physical problems. But the psychology of learning has no clear evidence to offer in favour of this approach.

Nor does research provide much support for the hypothesis that children learn to speak a foreign language more easily when they are young than when they are older, though there is plenty of anecdotal evidence. Indeed, a recent evaluation of the Nuffield-sponsored project for teaching French in primary schools, which was partly stimulated by this evidence, has cast some doubt on it.[3]

Further pitfalls become evident in the 'development' component of the RD and D model. Even if a development team has managed to set out an appropriate statement of its aims, and a teaching approach which relates to those aims, it then has to clothe its ideas in practical form. It has to decide which elements in the subject content are essential, and which peripheral. Alternatively, if it adopts the radical view that no particular topic is indispensable (as a group of history teachers might decide, say, that no one period is crucial for their purposes), then it has to consider which best suits the given educational requirements and is likely best to sustain the pupil's interests. There is, of course, considerable scope for judgement here, a scope which inevitably removes the development process from the realm of science into an art.

The trial stage is intended to compensate for any errors of judgement which might have occurred in the process of matching content to aims and approach. By trying out draft materials in the classroom and carefully collecting feedback information on what works and what does not, it should be possible to turn a working prototype into a satisfactory finished product. Undeniably, the process of trying out a new curriculum programme is useful to its developers, particularly on points of detail (whether a particular sequence is too difficult for pupils to follow, whether a specific passage is obscurely or ambiguously expressed, whether a particular topic fails to arouse a lively pupil response). However, it is very seldom the case (as many of the Schools Council evaluations show)[4] that evidence can be collected about how far the general aims of the programme are being achieved. Partly, this is because most trial stages are simply too short to enable the developers to stand back and take an overall view of the effects of the process. Partly, too, it can be a matter of the teachers' unfamiliarity with the notion of curricular objectives. Their reports on trials often give useful guidance on points of detail, but offer little in the way of critical comment on the overall design or on how far classroom practice can embody the developers' aims.

It is at the stage of 'diffusion', however, that the weaknesses of the RD and D approach are revealed most clearly. Many early development programmes assumed that, once a set of curricular materials had been perfected through trial and revision, and had been shown to work under classroom conditions, little remained to be done beyond making them widely available to schools through the usual channels of publishers, audio-visual suppliers and apparatus manufacturers. In most cases brief introductory courses were provided for interested teachers, explaining the background to and philosophy behind the development project, and running through a few typical classroom sequences: but these were seen as optional extras rather than as an integral part of the programme.

In the event, teachers did not respond in the logical way they were expected to do to the quality of the materials and the ideas underlying them. Often they were much slower to take up schemes than the developers predicted (for example, the PSSC Physics scheme rapidly attracted 10 per cent of its target audience, but even some ten years after its publication the adoption rate had only risen to about 18 per cent). Many of those who did adopt a particular scheme appeared to ignore, or misunderstand, or reject, the underlying values and philosophy of the developers. It was not uncommon to find science teachers using the predominantly open-ended Nuffield Science materials in a didactic way (dictating notes on experiments rather than having pupils carry them out), or language teachers using the predominantly oral-based Schools Council language materials to perpetuate the very grammar–translation approach which they had been designed to undermine. The classroom materials failed to carry the message: and this began to raise questions about whether they were really the appropriate medium after all.

At this point in the evolution of subject-based development (a point which appears to have been reached independently, and at different times, in one country after another) the validity of the RD and D approach began to be questioned. Critics pointed out that it embodied a highly technocratic set of assumptions. It assumed the existence of some central expertise not available to the average teacher (and sometimes – as in the case of most American science projects – demanding teams composed predominantly of university professors, despite their unfamiliarity with school conditions). It assumed that learning materials could be engineered in the way that a new household product could (the whole approach was based on a close analogy with the manufacturing process of new technological equipment). And above all, it assumed that knowledge was something that could be delivered in 'packages' (shipped out from some central point to an eager clientele), and was largely independent of personal interaction between teachers and taught.

The social-interaction strategy

Although these criticisms did not always fairly reflect the work of the development teams, there was enough truth in them to generate a strong reaction against the notion of 'teacher-proof' curriculum materials. It was argued that the attempt to bypass the teacher (by putting materials in the pupil's hands and assuming that these would provide more effective learning opportunities) was fundamentally misconceived. The real need was to involve classroom teachers much more in the business of curriculum reform, to encourage teachers to develop their own goals and strategies, assisted by suitable resources, rather than produce tightly structured packages geared to pre-determined objectives.

The alternative adopted was what Havelock describes as the social-interaction model; in Donald Schon's terminology,[5] this was the periphery–periphery model, as against the centre–periphery style of the original RD and D approach (in which a strong central organization, assumed to possess a monopoly of know-how, emitted instructions to practitioner groups at the periphery, and where communication was largely one-way and the structure of the system was hierarchical). Its first exemplars in the UK were in the field of the primary school curriculum, where teachers were more free to develop 'child-centred' approaches geared to the perceived needs and interests of individual pupils than in secondary schools with their various external constraints – especially the public examinations.

Developers, like the Nuffield Junior Science and Junior Mathematics teams, recognized that a tightly structured curriculum plan would be unacceptable. Piaget provided one reason: different pupils mature at different rates. Some are ready to acquire fundamental concepts, such as classification or conservation, before others of the same age. Secondly, local circumstances differ: if the content of study is to be linked to the pupils' own experience, then it may make sense in an urban classroom to introduce statistics by means of a traffic census, but a rural school may find it more appropriate to plot the distribution of wild flowers in a hedgerow.

The Nuffield Junior Science and Mathematics teams decided at the outset to concentrate on teachers rather than pupils. They intended to describe and elaborate on the best of existing practice, but codify it only enough to make it reasonably coherent, and to set up local networks of teachers who could then help each other to adapt and develop the results.

Thus, instead of being a highly expert materials-producing group (though its members have usually been as well-qualified in terms of knowledge and experience as their RD and D counterparts), the central team of the social-interaction model becomes a servicing agency drawing on, and disseminating, expertise which is already available in the system. Clearly defined curricular objectives for teaching particular subjects are no longer sought: it is assumed that teachers will determine their own goals, in relation to local circumstance. In consequence, published materials often provide no more than illustrative classroom activities for pupils, and focus predominantly on background information which the teachers themselves may require. The development process concentrates on finding ways whereby teachers may be helped to develop their own curricula.

The most noticeable difference between the RD and D and social-interaction models emerges in terms of dissemination. In the former, dissemination occurs almost as an afterthought; it is on the whole a peremptory affair, a matter of putting a few finishing touches to the overall design. In the latter, it is the central feature of the process, and everything else is subordinate to it.

The social-interaction model was an understandable reaction against what experience suggested to be the limitations of the RD and D process. But it, too, has important limitations.

The first concerns the neutrality of the central team. To reflect on (and perhaps amplify a little) the best of existing practice, even without introducing novel ideas, is to make judgements on what is the best. If its work is to have any coherence at all, a curriculum team will inevitably begin to form its own views and certain values and ideologies will be favoured at the expense of possible alternatives.

The second stage in the process is more crucial: namely, what the team does when it has surveyed the existing range of teaching ideas in the subject with which it is concerned. The project which pumps out information without processing it in any way, will be less potent than that which concentrates on building up a coherent set of resources and teaching suggestions, based on, but not limited to, examples of current practice.

This point can be illustrated in terms of the two instances already cited. Both relied on social-interaction techniques, but with very different results. The Nuffield Junior Mathematics Project developed an elaborate structure of topics. It used its trial schools to provide illustrations of ways of teaching new themes which it had itself introduced. Its publications, while directed at teachers rather than pupils, contained numerous examples of pupils' materials. It was, by any standards, an overall success. In contrast, the Nuffield Junior Science Project did not impose more than a rudimentary analytic framework on the material it collected. Its trial schools were not asked to do more than pick up one or two general topics which interested them. Its publications were more anecdotal in style and avoided being explicit about pupils' activities. In comparison with those of its mathematical counterpart, its results were disappointing. A similar approach in the secondary field, Project Technology (which again published a rather fragmentary series of examples of successful work in applied science), has also had a very limited success.

The device of the local teachers' network, brought together to undertake the detailed work of translating general curricular ideas into practical classroom terms, was an integral part of the strategy of the early social-interaction projects. Learning from the deficiencies of their RD and D counterparts, they concluded that teacher involyement must be a central component of the development process; how better to get them involved than by encouraging them to develop their own pupils' materials, within guidelines provided by the project team? A local teachers' group would, it was recognized, need to be stimulated and initially sustained by a flow of ideas and information which it was the team's business to channel (but not, in the purer version of the social-interaction model, to generate). It was assumed that, once the work of the local groups gathered momentum, it would need very little in the way of continuing support.

The instinct behind this move seems a sound one. Certainly, the stimulus which it has given to the in-service training of teachers (a theme too much neglected in the RD and D approach) has evoked a generally favourable response. But again drawbacks have emerged with experience. The enthusiasts who take part in local development activity are too few and their productions too unrepresentative of the ordinary teacher's needs for them to be focal points of development. Moreover, because their resources have been much more limited, the quality of what they have produced has tended to compare unfavourably with that of a well-funded RD and D project manned by a full-time team often recruited on a national basis.

Nor have local networks, once set up, proved to be self-sustaining. So long as they have had the impetus of a national project behind them they have usually flourished effectively enough; but once this outside support is withdrawn, they tend to disintegrate into small, isolated pockets of activists. (We shall return to the problem of sustaining interest in the results of development work in Chapter 8.)

Indeed, if it can be said that the main defect of the RD and D model is its excessive faith in the technocratic ideal, then it might equally be remarked that the social-interaction model is flawed by the romantic illusion. It assumes, falsely, that every teacher has the time, the talents and the motivation to take an active part in developing new teaching approaches and the classroom materials that go with them, and that he or she is prepared to put the necessary effort into contributing to a common pool of ideas and experience.

Perhaps the most obvious deficiency is time. To develop a highly sequential programmed text which students can work through largely on their own can demand at least forty hours of preparation for every hour of classroom use. But even compiling a set of resource materials to be used mainly as starting-points for teaching or learning will usually require a minimum of eight hours for every hour of eventual use. Although these estimates are of course very rough (because the complexity will vary with the subject-matter, the age of the pupils, and the extent to which the teacher demands active pupil participation) they give some indication of how unrealistic it is to assume that every teacher can 'do his own thing' in curriculum development, at least in the sense in which the term is normally used.

But it is also true that not every teacher, even if he or she had the time, would possess the necessary combination of skills to undertake an effective redesign of the traditional curriculum in a given subject for his or her pupils. The job requires a complex blend of creative imagination, technical expertise in ways of presenting information and ideas, a wide knowledge of the subject-matter, and an appreciation of the pupils' interests and the ways in which they can best be helped to learn – talents which are combined in few individuals. The team of a major curriculum development programme can be staffed by teachers chosen to contribute their several different skills and expertise: but the individual working largely on his own – even if reinforced and supported by a wealth of ideas and suggestions available through his local teachers' centre – will often find it too difficult as well as too time-consuming to translate an outline curriculum plan effectively into classroom practice.

Even where these barriers can be partly surmounted – by allowing teachers a part-time release from their normal classroom commitments, and providing them with some degree of specialized expertise in a teachers' centre – only a relatively small proportion of them will in practice want to involve themselves actively in the work of curriculum development. Many will be justifiably content to take the work done by others whose aims and approach they share, and to adapt it to their own particular circumstances – just as in the past they have been content to make their choice from the textbooks available, rather than feeling obliged to write their own.

Schon's periphery–periphery model assumes that local networks of teachers' centres, once stimulated into action by a central team, will continue not only to generate new ideas but to circulate these amongst themselves and to build up a common bank of curriculum resources. The network of Freinet schools in France[6] shows that this can be made to work where a central headquarters commissions materials from selected member groups, and even collects and publishes individual contributions where these are judged to be of sufficient quality and of sufficient relevance to the membership of the network as a whole. But most projects based on the social-interaction model lack this central source of leadership and collective responsibility once the central team has been disbanded. The main problem is that, within the structure of the educational system, there is no easy channel of lateral communication between one institution and another (whether at the level of the school, the teachers' centre or the local authority). Each institution normally communicates with its neighbour only by going through the next level up (school to school via the teachers' centre, centre to centre via the local authority, and authority to authority via the appropriate national organization). It is, in effect, something like travelling across England by train: very often, the easiest route is to go into London and out again.

A possible explanation for this lack of lateral connections is that the technology of education is very unstable. The social-interaction model works well in relation to products such as new drugs where, because their effectiveness can often be clearly established, the word passes rapidly round the periphery of the medical profession with relatively little mediation from the centre (though the influence of the professional journals, and of the sales force of the drug firm concerned, should not be overlooked). In education, in contrast, the effectiveness of any given approach will vary enormously from one situation to another. It cannot in any case be quickly or surely assessed. In consequence, there is no established tradition of rapid communication between practitioners in different localities; though as we shall see, the subject associations can play an important part in dissemination.

It is apparent then that the social-interaction approach, for all its differences from the RD and D model, shares with it a common deficiency. Both seriously underestimate the need for continuing follow-up, once the main development phase is over: the former in enabling teachers to understand the ideas behind the programme, and the latter (given that the ideas are implicit in the best of existing practice) in continuing to provide a channel by means of which new teaching approaches can be communicated.

The problem-solving approach

The third of the models can be seen as an attempt to cash in on the advantages and to minimize the snags which gradually became evident in both development strategies which preceded it. In Schon's terms, it represents a periphery–centre (rather than a centre–periphery or periphery–periphery) form of communication. It attempts to base itself firmly on the practitioner's needs; but it does not take the view that these can be met without substantial support from the centre.

The contrast can be pointed by considering the kind of materials produced by a central team adopting this type of approach. The RD and D team aimed to produce a comprehensive set of classroom materials, embodying a new curricular philosophy, sufficiently 'teacher-proof' to ensure that that philosophy could be effectively put into practice regardless of particular circumstances. In the social-interaction model the assumption was that the central team should produce materials to help the teacher rather than the pupils, not going too far beyond the current tradition, and leaving it to the teacher (either individually or through a local group) to translate the materials into classroom terms. In the problem-solving model, the emphasis reverts to pupils' materials, but these make no pretence to be comprehensive, and do not necessarily embody a particular pedagogic philosophy. The latter, it is assumed, must be developed by the teacher himself, perhaps after participation in an appropriate training programme.

Two contrasting examples of this problem-solving approach are provided by the Schools Council's Sixth Form General Studies Project and the Nuffield-sponsored Resources for Learning Project.

Both start by identifying a common teaching problem: in the case of the Sixth Form General Studies Project, this was the serious lack of classroom materials of good quality, both on topical themes and on fundamental issues, which confronts most teachers who attempt to introduce a 'broadening' element into the highly specialized curricula characteristic of sixth forms in England and Wales. The Project first set about trying to meet this deficiency by collecting together a 'bank' of items which practising teachers had devised for their own use, but which would, it was hoped, prove to be of more general relevance. A sophisticated and effective retrieval system was devised, with the idea that interested teachers could write or telephone for selected items which would meet their particular needs. Up to this point, the scheme bore a close resemblance to the social-interaction projects described above. But after a short period of experimentation with the 'item bank' approach, it became clear that more comprehensive sets of material would also be needed; so the Project team set about writing, and commissioning from outside authors, a series of study units grouped around certain major themes – contemporary economic and political issues, the problems of the environment, genetics and evolution, science and social responsibility, and so on. Each of these units was designed to occupy about a couple of hours' work, and could be used for either individual or group study. It was not essential that a teacher should be present for the whole period during which the material was used; a useful element of flexibility could, therefore, be introduced into the general studies timetable.

A special printing unit was set up near the team's headquarters in York. A standard format was worked out for the materials, which enabled each unit to be produced cheaply and quickly. The very low cost compensated for the fact that units were reproduced from type-script – though in fact the standard of presentation was reasonably high, and allowed for the inclusion of illustrations as well as text. The speed of production – often as little as four or five weeks from the completion of the manuscript to the date of the first publication – was especially important in bringing out highly topical material (for example, a unit analysing the spring 1974 general election campaign came out a very short time after the election itself). Schools could order materials through a subscription scheme which gave them an automatic entitlement to a given number of units of their choice.

Two main features of the General Studies Project serve to differentiate it from previous subject-based developments. First, the fact that its materials were not designed to provide a comprehensive 'package', but rather a series of short, adaptable units from which teachers could make their own selection, marks it off from the earlier RD and D programmes which aimed to develop major sections of the curriculum and to offer the results to teachers on a 'take-it-or-leave-it' basis. Secondly, these materials – though presented with much the same informal appearance as might characterize the products of a well-equipped teachers' centre – had behind them the editorial and design resources of an experienced full-time team. This distinguished them in quality from most pupils' materials generated by local networks in social-interaction projects.

The same two features were also characteristic of the work done in the later stages of the Nuffield Resources for Learning Project. Having identified a widespread need for materials which would help teachers to cope with mixed ability groups in comprehensive schools, the Project began to develop experimental units of materials for one particular age-group – thirteen-year-olds – in five subject areas – English, French, mathematics, science, and social studies. The team included one full-time editor/writer in each subject; it was found that each of the editor/writers was able to produce in a year enough independent learning units to service a year's work in the Project's trial schools. This was made possible only by the extensive use of existing materials, adapted as necessary. For example, the English units centred on a carefully chosen selection of paperbacks which students would find it useful to read in conjunction with their work. A variety of individual assignments were devised, based on these texts, which pupils might undertake as homework and as part of their classroom activities.

The relatively limited and small-scale trials of this approach were encouraging enough to merit a larger and more sustained programme; and in 1974 the Avon Local Education Authority, with a supporting grant from the Department of Education and Science, embarked on a scheme on broadly similar lines, to supply independent learning resources for pupils between the ages of eleven and sixteen in the same five subject areas.

Appraising the three developmental styles

The problem-solving approach to subject-based development may, in the event, provide a way of meeting many of the difficulties associated with earlier models. Its deliberately adaptable materials allow room for initiative by the teacher if he wishes to take it, but do not presuppose that he is willing to do all the work of curriculum development himself. The contrast between this and the earlier approaches can be brought out by an analogy. If you want a bookshelf, you can of course select one from the ready-made range in the furniture shop (the RD and D model). Or you can make it yourself, armed only with some planks of wood, a tool kit and perhaps a 'do-it-yourself' manual (the social-interaction model). Or you can send away for an assembly kit in which the various parts, and the types of finish, can be specified by the customer, who assembles the product himself but has a good deal of the preliminary work done for him (the problem-solving model).

There are, nevertheless, some limitations which can already be recognized in this third, relatively recent, development strategy. In its emphasis on producing materials to meet teachers' existing needs, and leaving them to put their own interpretations on such materials, it goes along with the current teaching traditions rather than attempting to make any radical changes to them. It shares, in other words, the conservative assumptions of the social-interaction model, rather than the potentially more radical possibilities offered by the RD and D approach. In designing its materials to be all things to all men, it misses the opportunity – more readily taken by the social-interaction approach – to link curriculum development more closely to in-service training. Again, the open-ended nature of its materials makes them difficult to evaluate and hence to revise and progressively to improve.

The main difficulty is, however, embodied in the very conception of a problem-solving approach. Ideally, such an approach should imply a close investigation of each client school's particular needs, and the specific working out of a solution geared to those needs. In fact, resources for curriculum development in the foreseeable future are likely to be far too limited for such a close client–consultant relationship between development teams and individual schools or teachers. The whole business would be much too labour-intensive (just as psychoanalysis is too labour-intensive to offer a realistic solution to mental illness). So a compromise has to be reached in which the problems identified, and the solutions designed for them, are general rather than specific. Though such projects try to build in adaptability, not all the intended clients will necessarily be accurate in assessing their real requirements, or in matching them with the materials provided. Some of them may also find it difficult to make the right kind of modifications to these materials to ensure that they can do an effective educational job in the context of the classroom.

A brief summary of the three main approaches to subject-based development discussed in this chapter is contained in Table 2 (the fifth and sixth rows anticipate the discussion of dissemination and evaluation in Chapters 8 and 9 below).[7] This is intended only as a sketchy caricature; such sharp distinctions do not exist, nor do the three overall categories themselves – however helpful they may be in establishing general relationships between different modes of curriculum development – give more than a very over-simplified account of the complex range of subject-based projects. In practice, many schemes overlap, or fall between, the categories we have attempted to define. For example, one of the most interesting – and in some ways most far-reaching – programmes, the Humanities Curriculum Project, has features of all three. It has produced substantial 'blocks' of classroom material, in RD and D style; but each package looks more like a 'resource pack' in the problem-solving genre; and there is also, as in the social-interaction approach, a strong emphasis on teacher development organized on a regional basis.

Indeed, the best future for subject-based development may lie in a judicious amalgam of all three strategies, rather than in an over-concentration on any one. In every systematic attempt to improve the quality of education, there is likely to be some tension between the centre and the periphery. The periphery (the client schools and teachers) has a variety of different needs, but lacks the resources to provide adequately for them. But if the centre, the development team, attempts in any standardized way to meet these needs, it tends to get out of touch with the realities of the individual classroom and to alienate or confuse many of its potential clients. If the periphery then decides to go it alone, the resulting innovations are usually limited in scale, uneconomic, and may be of poor quality. They are

Table 2   *Curriculum development styles*

	Cluster I Instrumental	Cluster II Interactive	Cluster III Individualistic
View of knowledge	Packages (subject disciplines)	Problems (interdisciplinary inquiry)	Personal exploration (eclectic searches)
Categories of goal emphasized	Job/career	Social adjustment	Personal happiness
Means adopted	Highly structured materials	Loosely structured (but researched) materials	Unstructured (non-existent?) materials
Teachers' classroom roles	Dominating	Managing	Assisting
Dissemination strategies	Teachers as passive (rational) recipients	Teachers as representative (token?) participants	Teachers as (partial?) developers
Evaluation techniques	Attainment of pre-specified goals	Anthropological ('illuminative') studies	Individual case-histories
View of humanity	People as things (manipulable)	People as social animals	People as individuals
View of external reality	*Terra firma* (the real world)	Sandbanks (the changing world)	*Terra incognita* (the unknowable, therefore unknown)
	Newton?	Einstein?	Berkeley?

also liable to be excessively dependent on the enthusiasm of individuals and so to lack staying power. The answer to this dilemma could well be for the centre to develop a variety of solutions to common problems, which allow the periphery to make the final choice but leave ample scope for local adaptation.

Such a composite approach, however, demands an educated consumer: one who can, with limited outside support, express his own autonomy and make his own intelligent decisions. This in its turn poses a recurring need for the professional development of teachers; and indeed for the active involvement of all the agents of traditional development. It is to this consideration, among others, that we shall turn in Chapter 8 in discussing some of the problems of dissemination.

6 System-based development

Changing the contents and teaching methods of individual subjects – subject-based development – may be achieved within a single subject department of a school. But changing the system – the structure or aims of schools – will affect the nature of teaching and learning across the whole board, because (as we argued earlier) the curriculum in its wide sense is closely bound up with the organization and policy of schools. System-based curriculum development may go beyond the individual school, to involve a larger sub-system such as a local authority, and at its most wide-ranging the entire national educational policy for which the government's minister of education is responsible.

It may take two forms. One, external development, reflects certain social goals and hopes by translating these into changes in educational organization and structure to make the schools work more effectively in achieving these goals. The other, internal development, is rather the expression of a 'grass roots' movement among practising teachers than the result of electioneering chickens coming home to roost; it can usually be related to some shift in underlying educational values or philosophy, and its impact is primarily on the day-to-day practices of the classroom.

External forms of system-based change

Habit and tradition impose a comfortable inertia on the educational system; structural reform therefore requires the use of legislative pressure from outside. It is hardly surprising that the political energy needed for this tends to derive from clear ideological notions of what society ought to be about. Those, however, who see education primarily as a means for promoting social ends may well fail to acknowledge and spell out the curricular implications of the organizational changes they favour. By stopping halfway they may create a situation of muddle and uncertainty. The schools will have a natural tendency to struggle on with the old familiar curriculum, but now inside a framework which fails adequately to accommodate it.

Some countries are more consistent than others in following through the curricular logic of structural innovations. France and Sweden, for example, usually accompany proposals for new structures with detailed recommendations at the classroom level, but in England and Wales the link between organizational and curricular reform is recognized only covertly. The contrast may be exemplified by the methods adopted in these countries to foster an aim most European nations have established in recent years: to reduce social class divisions and promote equal educational opportunities.

Reforms on this egalitarian, anti-élitist theme have concentrated on the transition from primary to secondary education. Traditional types of secondary school were judged to reinforce – or at least to perpetuate – existing social class divisions. Those who urge greater social equality have sought to defer any differentiation of the curriculum between the academic (predominantly middle-class) and non-academic (predominantly working-class) pupils until as late a stage as possible. In a number of countries the result has been the complete or partial reorganization of the secondary school system on comprehensive lines. In others, common 'bridge years' have been introduced between the primary and the secondary stage, or new middle schools have been set up to postpone the secondary selection process until the age of thirteen, fourteen or fifteen.

In Sweden the changeover to comprehensive education was achieved through a carefully planned programme, beginning with a series of monitored experiments affecting only a limited number of schools. The main consequences of the reform were as far as possible anticipated and provided for: changes in organization were matched by changes in subject content, and also to some extent by teacher training and the production of teaching materials. The same consistency and coordination was applied to the relations between one part of the system and another. The upper secondary schools were reorganized to take account of the introduction of the nine-year comprehensive school from seven to sixteen; a few years later the reform of higher education was put in hand to accommodate the consequences of the reorganized *gymnasium*. At each turn, the planning decisions were accompanied by development and training programmes; development was clearly seen as part of the total exercise of policy negotiation and policy-making.

No less committed to system-based development are the French, carrying through a reform of secondary education which aims to postpone differentiation into academic and technical streams until about the age of fourteen, and re-plan the curriculum for the early years of the secondary school. They use traditional instruments: the Inspectorate, aided by a newly established system of regional documentation centres; revision of the curricular guidelines for the schools; the modification of the examinations. It would be possible to split hairs about how far such system-based change is developmental; it relies heavily on the network of shared assumptions within the system, and the expertise of an élite group commanding professional respect as well as titular authority. The scale is much larger than that of Sweden; the educational tradition is less influenced by North American models; the system is less susceptible to neat and clear-cut planning; it contains within it more tensions. But the central concern is nevertheless with system-wide change and the development of appropriate forms of organization, teaching methods and content.

These countries recognized the directly educational effects of socio-political reforms – that, for example, mixed ability grouping (which is a logical outcome of a policy of desegregation) implies changes in both teaching aims and classroom practice.

At the other extreme, efforts in England and Wales to abolish the eleven-plus selection procedures and amalgamate the various types of secondary schools were patchy and haphazard. Political protagonists of comprehensive education represented it as a mere change of administrative arrangement with no curricular strings attached; within the existing structure of academic rewards (the CSE, O and A Level examinations, university entrance and the rest), it was argued, everyone would benefit and nobody would lose as more pupils, from wider social backgrounds, would advance further along the road to academic success. This tendency to play down the connection between organizational reform and the need for curricular reappraisal may stem in part from a temperamental distrust of *a priori* reasoning; in part also it derives from the *de facto* control teachers have acquired over their own curricular actions and the limited role of the Department of Education and Science. This has entailed that for the most part the curricular consequences of comprehensive reforms, undertaken piecemeal, have unfolded slowly, and have had to be worked out by individual schools as best they can. 'The freedom of the teacher' has often precluded collective action between schools even within the same local authority area. True, traditional agents have been brought in, notably the HMIs, who provided a range of courses and seminars on secondary school management and offered what amounted to a consultancy service to l.e.a.s on the managerial problems of transition from selective to non-selective secondary organization. But the contrast with Sweden or France is strong.

Other European countries again provide examples of strategies by which external system-based change can be experimentally tested so that initial ideas can be reappraised – a necessary part of an organized process. In the Netherlands a small designated group of innovative schools was used to explore the possibilities of introducing a comprehensive middle school for all pupils from twelve to sixteen. The plan provided for five schools a year for three years (starting in 1976) to move over to a fully or partly comprehensive intake and for a larger group of thirty-nine schools to be associated with the scheme as 'resonance' schools – that is, schools which would act as a sounding-board for the ideas coming out of the pilot group and would help to draw lessons from their experience.

A full-time 'innovation committee' was appointed to coordinate the scheme. Extra resources were provided for each of the project schools (equivalent to about half a dozen extra staff members) and support services were offered by curriculum development agencies and advisory staff. One departure from normal Dutch practice was that the responsibility for the preparation of new curricula was placed on the teaching staff of the project schools, not on an external planning agency, though it was the intention in due course to issue general curricular guidelines on the basis of the work carried out in the schools. This readiness to locate some of the essential development work at the school face may in the end prove the most significant aspect of the plan.

Even so, many difficulties have to be overcome. The sub-system, valuable as it may be as an arena for experiment, cannot resolve problems which are national problems. In the case of the Netherlands, the present secondary structure is divided into four strands, with the traditional grammar school at one end and the secondary modern at the other. At the age of twelve, pupils sort themselves out among the various separate types of school, on the basis of guided choice. The new experimental middle schools are enjoined to broaden the subject-matter of instruction, individualize teaching and learning, and develop social awareness. The more ambitious among them are also trying to devise a unified curriculum for the years from twelve to sixteen which can meet the needs of all pupils, while at the same time preparing some of them adequately for the next, post-compulsory, stage of education.

Clearly, however, these schools – even though strongly supported by the national authorities – cannot be expected to change the constraints which bear upon them from outside, such as the demands of post-secondary education or the competitive pressures of other schools still operating on a traditional basis. More important still, they cannot change the structure of the Netherlands' teaching profession, which is split up according to the present divisions of secondary education – a separate training, salary scale and promotion ladder for the teachers in each type of secondary school. Though there are obvious benefits in setting up a pilot unit, separated from the main education system for the purposes of development, the Dutch example serves also as a reminder that the unit's very separateness and departure from typicality can distract attention from basic and system-wide issues, and thus introduce its own distortions.

Could England have used a similar strategy? One possibility might have been to put extra resources into pilot schools in difficult areas, as part of an action research programme for comprehensive education. Such a programme – assuming it were freed of the limitations of short-term finance – might have provided a useful way of developing individual institutions, while at the same time maintaining a regular reporting and evaluation procedure to make sure that the lessons learnt should be available to the system as a whole.

Another alternative might have taken the form of topic-based development groups. Some schools might, for instance, have co-operated in exploring the differing effects of different sizes of organizational unit, and in working out how best to divide a large pupil population into more manageable academic and social groups. Others might have pooled their know-how on mixed ability teaching, or collaborated in the development of materials for independent learning. Yet others might have concentrated on the issues of the common-core curriculum and on ways of helping to ensure that the least able did not fall through the cultural net.

It would be part and parcel of such arrangements that each school concerned in the programme would no longer be tackling its educational tasks in isolation, but would be connected with a wider network of institutions in which ideas could be shared and collectively developed. This would of course involve, if not a call on additional resources, then at least a reallocation of existing resources, so as to

release teaching staff (along with Inspectors and advisers) to participate in the work of support teams for collaborating groups of
schools.

Internal forms of system-based change

So far we have been concerned with what we termed 'external'
system-based development. We distinguished also another form,
'internal' development, deriving from changes in educational philosophy or advances in classroom practice, or (more usually) a combination of the two. Its distinctive emphases are on relationships and
processes, rather than on political aims and structures.

The progressive movement in English primary schools is an
illustrative example. Certainly Piaget and Dewey were called in as
ex post facto apologists, but its origins lay rather in changing approaches to child-rearing and the growth of permissive attitudes
within family and social relationships over several generations. In
the educational context this basic shift in values brought about a
variety of quite substantial curriculum reforms, though the new
ideas took a long time to percolate and their effects were variable and
uncertain. Changes spread upwards from the nursery school and
kindergarten, through the infant to the junior school. Once it began
to be generally accepted that the primary curriculum should be
dominated as much by the needs of the growing child as by society's
requirements that he or she should learn to read, write and count,
pupils were encouraged to develop a wide range of skills besides those
of literacy and numeracy. They were given more opportunity to
pursue their own creative interests and talents through art, handi-
craft, drama and movement and to discover and enjoy a diversity of
physical activities.

Although the curricular goals were seldom made explicit, the
tendency was to shift from competition to cooperation as the main
social objective, and to replace didactic and directive teaching
methods with an approach which allowed children a large measure
of choice in their day-to-day activities. In many schools the internal
organization became less formal and the structure was adapted to
encourage active, interest-based learning. In a number of instances
absence of a formal timetable and the lack of closely organized class
groups led to demands for an open-plan pattern of architecture which
could allow still greater flexibility in the school's working day.

These changes were not the result of deliberate, centrally

controlled efforts. The eleven-plus examination, before it was dismantled in the process of secondary school reform, was never used as an instrument for development in primary schools, though it did provide a constraint on them (indeed its only national unity lay in the fact that most local authorities used tests provided by institutions such as the National Foundation for Educational Research and Moray House). Traditional processes did operate, in that HMIs, in their capacity as advisers, propagated a liberal orthodoxy in innumerable encounters with individual teachers in the course of visitation and with groups of teachers in the provision of refresher courses. Moreover, five HMIs were directly associated with the work of the Plowden committee,[1] including J. F. M. Blackie who afterwards wrote a popular guide, *Inside the Primary School* (HMSO, 1967), which projected the committee's optimistic view of informal education.

Publishers of books for children and for the primary school market have noted the character of this prevailing orthodoxy, and the 1960s saw a remarkable extension of the range of publications, including children's paperbacks. Class libraries have become a familiar feature of primary schools. The attempt has been made to diversify the reading schemes used, and extend the variety of well-illustrated fiction and non-fiction at the disposal of children and teachers.[2]

But the development was essentially unplanned: the organizational structure permitted it to happen, but it was nobody's business to see that any particular reform was introduced, and much of the impetus came through individuals and individual schools. The virtue of this freedom was that it inspired a high level of personal commitment in many of the teachers. (In contrast, American experience shows how difficult it is to transport, lock, stock and barrel across the Atlantic, a new teaching style depending on changed teacher attitudes and priorities which cannot be imposed by technocratic methods. The home-grown American equivalent, if it could be identified, could not be the same as any available English export.)

The part played by Chief Education Officers and advisers in generalizing and spreading new curricular ideas at the primary level has already been remarked upon in Chapter 4. Vital as it has been, it remains intensely personal and idiosyncratic. It defies all the developmental metaphors drawn from engineering and invites images from horticulture and the pastoral pursuits. Innovation has to be seeded and cultivated. Teachers whose work has appeared to their professional and administrative colleagues to be worth propagating are carefully nurtured; their effectiveness is multiplied by choosing fertile places to plant them out. Good schools serve as breeding-grounds for candidates for responsible posts elsewhere.

The pressure behind the innovation was the moral force of scores of individual innovators. But perhaps the process of personal inter-action by which change was disseminated was the only one appro-priate to curricular innovation based on a shift in teacher attitudes. The change in the schools had more to do with the change in the teachers' self-image than with the rational application of research or the fully tested introduction of new teaching techniques.

The progressive primary movement, then, provides an instance in which the process of change characteristic of external system-based development is reversed. Where its ideals are fully realized, internal reform, deriving from a shift in basic educational values, brings about direct changes in the pattern of teaching and learning and in curricular aims. These in their turn can eventually affect the organi-zation and even the architecture of the school and the functioning of the system as a whole. The overall structure is shaped by the curriculum, rather than the curriculum being constrained by the structure.

The way in which change has spread, however, has made its effects so uneven that nobody can say with assurance how widespread is the use of informal teaching methods, or its associated techniques such as vertical grouping (in which children from different age-groups work together) or the integrated day (in which the traditional time-table for separate subjects gives place to an open and flexible arrangement exploiting the pupils' own developing interests). The Plowden committee, despite the assistance of a survey by HMIs, was not able to offer a clear estimate of the prevalence of methods which were, in any case, not defined with any precision; however, it shared the general conviction of other writers of the late 1960s that between a quarter and a third of all primary schools demonstrated these informal qualities. But Dr Neville Bennett's subsequent investi-gation of teaching styles in the north-west of England in 1974 suggested that according to a rigorous application of Plowden prin-ciples the proportion of informal primary schools in Lancashire and Cumbria was less than one in ten.[3] He also found a wide range of 'mixed' informal–formal schools which combined some charac-teristic progressive and traditional methods. At the other end of the spectrum, about 25 per cent of schools fell into the formal category. These figures depended on the particular typology which Bennett developed, and the practice of teaching does not necessarily lend itself to the neat application of such typological divisions. What can hardly be disputed is the wide range of styles and methods which exist alongside one another and the limited extent to which it is possible to speak of the English 'system' of primary education, or of any clearly describable system-based change which would characterize its curriculum as a whole.

In Chapter 3 we remarked how this loose organization has been criticized on the grounds that the 'public' curriculum has thereby disintegrated, and how some critics have urged that 'standards' should be resurrected in the shape of a minimum required level of attainment at specified ages between five and fifteen. The Assessment of Performance Unit established within the Department of Education and Science in the mid-1970s was instructed to devise and apply measures of scholastic performance which, by means of light sampling techniques, can provide regular indices of school attainment at various ages, so as to enable the Secretary of State to answer questions about rising or falling standards in the schools.

These testing procedures have not been intended as an instrument of centrally controlled curriculum development. But, in fact, if the reappraisal of informal primary education in Britain is to be turned to good advantage (rather than used as a weapon to destroy the inventive confidence of a great many individual schools and teachers) it may be very important to harness the critical energy of activists within the educational system more efficiently than before, and to organize system-based curriculum change on a more coherent pattern. And this means, among other things, admitting constraints on the teacher's freedom of action, and using the instruments of control as a positive means of development.

The effects of internal changes are slow, sporadic and patchy: the grass roots, if not carefully tended, can fail to grow into a tidy lawn – and in any case the shoots take a long time to appear. The absence of centralized planning means that most schools have in practice to resolve their own curricular problems. This can be wasteful; it is also, if it goes too far, at odds with the idea of system-based change, which implies some attempt at least to view education as a *system*.

But internal changes have one great advantage over external ones: they are embedded in the reality of the classroom rather than in the rhetoric of the reformers. Unless a change in organization is such that teachers can themselves accept the rationale behind it, they may do no more than go through the motions necessary to comply with the new regime, and may in consequence undermine its real intention. And unless the practical implications of the reform can be worked out adequately in advance – whether through a pilot project or by some other means – it may prove difficult to implement in classroom terms, or may turn out in some unforeseen respect to do more educational harm than good.

In effect there is a choice, in system-based development, between two main alternatives. The first depends on generating a widespread change in the basic attitudes and professional beliefs of individual teachers, and so affecting – though to a limited and unpredictable degree – the whole tone of teaching and learning. The second is based on bringing about a legislated reform in the structure of some distinct part of the educational system, so designed as to realize certain clear goals, but not necessarily impinging in any significant way on teachers' styles and outlooks.

For obvious reasons, what we have called external forms of change are more characteristic of centralized than of decentralized educational systems – those in which the mechanisms of curricular control and development are highly articulated, and where it is part of the accepted tradition that schools should act at the bidding of the national legislature. Conversely, internal forms of change are more likely to occur in decentralized systems, or at least those which put a considerable premium on teacher freedom. But there are plenty of examples to belie a too-ready equation, and to show (as in the Freinet schools in France and the local comprehensive schools in Germany) that it remains possible within a formally centralized structure for enterprising groups of teachers to develop their own ideas.

7 Fragmentation and integration

The concept of the curriculum, as we analysed it in Chapter 1, seems far removed from the untidy actuality of most schools, whether primary or secondary, British or Belgian. One long tradition, deriving perhaps from the eighteenth-century encyclopedists, sees education as a holistic, unitary, and continuously evolving process – a steady unfolding of the seamless cloak of knowledge. The practical reality, in contrast, shows the schools as capable at best of producing a patchwork quilt, and at worst of generating a worthlessly fragmented collection of rags and tatters.

Educational planners, especially perhaps those in centrally controlled systems, have tried to make coherent the curriculum provided for children during the years of compulsory schooling. The Swedish system, for example, implicitly assumes that a complete, balanced and integrated diet can be produced if the necessary ingredients are combined with a given set of purposes in view.

But attempts to work from general goals to specific objectives have seldom given rise to a well-integrated curriculum. It is difficult to reach a consensus about the aims of education, even in a relatively close-knit community. When this has been done, it is never a straightforward matter of deduction to proceed from any broad statement of aims to the specific objectives of each curricular component. It is equally hard to translate such objectives into the particularities of day-to-day classroom activity. In practice, at the end of this dubious process of derivation, the constituent elements of the curriculum seem as fragmented as those they were carefully designed to replace. It is as if the very operation of dividing the complex whole into more manageable parts removes from it some of its essential character – as if education's vital spirit necessarily evaporates in the curriculum analyst's crucible.

It is easier to point out the difficulties of what is sometimes grandly called 'rational curriculum planning by objectives' than to suggest a satisfactory alternative. Fragmentation arises as a direct consequence of one of the most noticeable features of any school system: the way in which it erects barriers, both horizontal ones between educational stages and vertical ones between one curricular strand and another. If the divisions created by the differing abilities of the students themselves are also taken into account it may well seem as if the idea of a unified curriculum is forever doomed to suffer the death of a thousand cuts.

Barriers between different educational stages

Pupils may have to overcome a number of difficulties in making the transition from primary to secondary schools (and, to a lesser extent, from infant to junior, and from lower to upper secondary levels). A year-group of primary pupils will characteristically be taught by a single general practitioner across the whole range of the curriculum; whereas a secondary year-group will be taught by several specialists in a series of distinct subjects. This contrast is reinforced by the teachers' own training, which is, in the majority of West European countries (as it was until comparatively recently in Britain), carried out in separate institutions. Many secondary teachers have university degrees and limited pedagogic training; on the other hand, few primary teachers are graduates, and their professional education stresses teaching methods rather than specialized subject content.

In an effort to reduce the traumata of adapting from one stage to the other some junior schools deliberately introduce an element of specialist teaching (whether in mathematics or a language or perhaps elementary science) in the final year or two; and some secondary schools attempt to postpone the introduction of specialization in such subjects as English, history, geography or religious education until after the first year at least. But the scope for adjustments of this kind is inevitably limited by the different backgrounds of the teachers. Because those with a primary training have been brought up to be class teachers, it is not easy for them to tackle a specialized assignment in the teaching of one subject to several different classes. Equally, because those with secondary qualifications have been brought up as specialists, it is not easy for them to tackle a generalist assignment in the teaching of several different subjects to one class.

The discontinuities may be reduced by bringing together gene-ralists and specialists within a single organizational framework – as in the 'middle schools' of the UK, or the 'years of orientation' in

France or the Netherlands – but they cannot altogether be elimi-
nated. Indeed, yet another set of frontiers may be interposed for the
pupil to negotiate. As a distinct middle school tradition emerges,
the teachers concerned will inevitably develop a sense of their own
identity, subtly different from that which characterizes the staffs of
the first schools; and (in much the way that infant and junior
teachers, even within the same relatively small institutions, hold
themselves distinct) the lines of communication will weaken across
the boundaries.

At the age when compulsory schooling ends (now sixteen-plus in
many countries in Western Europe, though it remains at fifteen-plus
in a number of Mediterranean countries) another very obvious
discontinuity occurs. The post-compulsory curriculum usually offers
more options and demands more specialization than that which
precedes it. Students who choose to stay on at school after the
statutory leaving age are expected – rightly or wrongly – to have a
clearer idea of what they are good at and what they want to do; and
many of them are likely to be preparing themselves for entry to
higher education.

When they move into the tertiary level they again meet teachers
with a different status and self-image, and face a new degree of
specialization, new teaching methods and new learning styles. Sixth-
form colleges and sixth-form work in further education have pur-
ported to reduce the gulf between school and university, or (in some
ways a more ambitious claim) between school and the world outside.
But in reality, their provision of courses is often made more for
economic than for educational reasons (many of the smaller comprehensive schools could only sustain a whole range of sixth-form
provision at excessive cost). Once introduced, however, separate
sixteen-plus institutions do create an opportunity for their teachers
to experiment with more sophisticated teaching styles, to give the
students greater responsibility for their own learning, and to develop
a more adult atmosphere than is possible in an 'all through' eleven-
to-eighteen school.

Variations in curricular practice between one educational level
and the next make the hurdles more difficult to leap. For example,
it may so happen that one youngster begins mathematics in the infant
school in a concrete way by classifying and sorting objects, cutting
out shapes and the like; that he or she is then taught computation
formally in the junior school in terms of learning tables by rote
and manipulating complex arithmetical calculations; that in the

secondary school the curricular style reverts to a more active, discovery-based mode in which the emphasis is on unifying concepts such as sets, transformations and other aspects of 'new mathematics'; and that in the sixth-form college there is a different concern with applied topics and with computer science. For such a pupil, it could hardly be said that the school system had managed to present any very coherent view of the discipline or had made it particularly easy to learn.

Another problem is posed by repetition of material – perhaps more noticeably in the so-called 'non-linear' disciplines (English, history, geography and so on). Until recently it was a favourite tactic in school history to begin with the Roman invasion of Britain – and thus with a background sketch of Ancient Rome – before moving on chronologically over the intervening nineteen centuries to the present day. Sometimes an enthusiastic infant school teacher would introduce a project on Julius Caesar; one or more of the junior school teachers would in all likelihood do the same; so that by the time the pupils reached secondary school they would be 'doing' the Romans for the third time. Perhaps there is no great harm for a pupil to return to the same theme again and again; but certainly time may be wasted when the same ground is covered more than twice, and a child may well be bored by over-familiar material.

A different problem arises from the fact that pupils usually come to a secondary school from a wide variety of primary schools. Even if a certain topic is familiar to the majority, there will almost inevitably be one or two who have never come across it before. Without a centrally determined curriculum it is virtually impossible for the teacher to make any assumptions about what is common knowledge for his or her class. Another side of the same coin is presented by the pupil whose family moves from one area to another, and who therefore has to change schools at other than the usual points of transfer. In countries where the rate of population mobility is approaching 10 per cent per annum, this strengthens the case for those who argue for a nationally defined curricular provision, or at least a strong 'common core'.

And yet, despite the discontinuities between one level and another, the school systems in highly decentralized countries (such as England and Wales) show no signs of breaking down. This may in part be ascribed to the facility of the human mind in adapting itself from one set of circumstances to another, in picking up new habits and tricks of thought, and in bridging substantial gaps in knowledge by indirect inference. But another reason why the barriers between institutions do not cause as much trouble as one might expect is that the diversity of curricular practice in a decentralized system usually conceals a sizeable consensus. This underlying unity (as we have seen in Chapters 3 and 4) has been maintained both by the requirements of national examinations at the secondary stage and by the availability of textbooks.

Barriers between different curricular subjects

Another source of curricular fragmentation lies in the divisions between different subject disciplines. At the primary school level this is scarcely a problem: and it should be noted why it is not. The whole organization of the school, and the whole professional preparation of the teachers, militates against making sharp distinctions between, say, geography and biology or mathematics and English language. By and large, each class stays with a single teacher throughout the school year, and that teacher has no strong claim to disciplinary allegiance. In contrast, the separation of subjects is built into the very structure of the secondary school: the timetable is constructed out of discrete building blocks (one period for history, two for physics, and so on); many of the classrooms – and all the laboratories – represent specialized territory; and the staff are organized in subject departments which compete strongly for a major share of both time-table time and teaching space.

An interesting and suggestive set of distinctions has been developed by Professor Basil Bernstein.[1] He adopts a sociological perspective on the way in which knowledge is classified and transmitted, and is concerned primarily with the contrast between 'integrated' and 'collection' curricula – the former corresponding roughly to the tradition of the more progressive among English primary schools, and the latter to the tradition of the more academic among English secondary schools.

Bernstein's analysis distinguishes between two main elements in 'the educational knowledge code' – namely, 'classification' and 'framing'. Classification is a measure of how strong the boundaries are between one given set of contents and another, and how far there is division of labour between those who transmit the contents in question. Thus, an 'integrated' curriculum is characterized by weak classification and a 'collection' curriculum by strong. The notion of framing relates to a different, though connected, issue: 'the degree of control teacher and pupil possess over the selection, organisation, pacing and timing of the knowledge transmitted and received . . .' Strong framing entails relatively few curricular options; weak framing allows a considerable range of them. The two elements are, in principle, independent of one another; in practice they often go together. Thus, academic secondary school courses are characterized both by strong classification and relatively strong framing, and primary courses by weak classification and weak framing. However, there are also intermediate categories – especially at the tertiary level – such as rigorously designed interdisciplinary studies (weak classification but strong framing) or specialized unit-credit courses (strong classification but weak framing).

In terms of Bernstein's categories, it can readily be seen that the 'system-based' strategies for heuristic development discussed in Chapter 6 are both a product of, and a means of perpetuating, educational systems based on integrated curricula; and similarly, that the 'subject-based' strategies for heuristic development discussed in Chapter 5 are both a product of, and a means of perpetuating, educational systems based on collection curricula.

The more radical critics of secondary schooling argue that the division of the curriculum into separate subjects is élitist (and therefore culpable) as well as unnecessary. The schools have no cause to reflect the structure of the universities (which has itself evolved largely as a result of historical accident): in doing so, they merely show their excessive and disproportionate concern with that small minority of privileged pupils destined for higher education. What is needed, rather, is a curriculum shaped by the world outside the school, centred upon the real problems which pupils will subsequently encounter (social violence, overpopulation, environmental pollution) and the real skills which they will subsequently be called upon to exercise (deciding how to vote, knowing the law, being aware of welfare entitlements, cooperating with others on a given task).

Such radicals can counter-attack on two fronts the argument in favour of the established disciplines which contends that the different forms of disciplinary training are not so much ends in themselves – ways of equipping people to solve specialized problems within, say, history, mathematics or biology – as complementary means of developing 'a trained mind'.

First, there is very little firm evidence that what is called 'transfer of training' actually takes place.[2] In other words, just because someone is able to exercise a skill in one context (e.g. being a good Monopoly player), it does not mean that he or she will automatically deploy that skill to good effect in another (e.g. being a successful property developer). Remarkably few people seem in fact to be good at practising in a wide context what they preach in a specialized one: child psychiatrists surprisingly often have disturbed children, social workers frequently have difficult domestic lives, and teacher trainers are not always outstanding at communicating ideas. So perhaps the teaching of science because it encourages powers of observation in relation to laboratory experiments is not, after all, justifiable in terms of promoting a general facility to observe with more than usual accuracy.

Secondly, the critics point with unkindly devastating effect to the competitive acquisitiveness of the separate disciplines. Every group of subject-matter experts – be they physicists, geographers or art teachers – is concerned to lay claim to the maximum number of desirable goals for their teaching. Thus, if the encouragement of powers of observation is held to be a general good, then the physicists will assert that this is what physics fosters. But the geographers or the art teachers – or, for that matter, the biologists or the historians – will make the same point in favour of their subjects. If all the different school subjects which claim to inculcate a respect for evidence or to develop powers of analysis, or to enhance the pupil's capability for communication, actually do so, then the curriculum is grossly redundant and could be pruned with obvious advantage.

This rivalry reflects the fact that academic subjects enjoy a socio-political entity in their own right. They represent powerful interest groups, legitimated and given sanction not only by the qualifications which they award, but also by the fact that publishers' lists and library catalogues faithfully reflect the categories which they impose. The secondary curriculum can be seen as a territory carved up and balkanized into a series of separate empires over which the more powerful disciplines hold sway. Operating mainly from a series of bases within higher education, they seek to colonize and inculcate the secondary schools with their values and their forms of thought – mainly by means of sending missionary graduates into the heathen hinterland. Usually, the primary schools remain innocent of their penetration; because too remote from the conquering homeland, they are seldom deemed worthy of assault.

When appraised from the God's-eye view of the sociologist or political scientist, the stoutly defended claims of the subject specialist

T.P.O.C.C.—D

may often sound naïvely self-seeking. And yet it may be equally simple-minded to fall into a knowing cynicism, as some of Bernstein's less distinguished acolytes have been prone to do. One can easily end up in the quaint position of implying that the whole of organized knowledge is based on a vast conspiracy, in which one group of people describing themselves as mathematicians arbitrarily carve up their own slice of reality while another, calling themselves specialists in German literature, with comparable capriciousness carve up another, and so on. This dialogue can easily be brought to an end with a piece of knock-down logic. It is self-contradictory to use arguments based on one disciplinary framework – that of sociology – to dispute the legitimacy of *all* arguments based on disciplinary frameworks.

Meanwhile, more traditionally-minded proponents of the educational status quo point out that the different established disciplines do in fact have a basis in logic as well as a rationale within the social and political context of primary, secondary and tertiary institutions. They embody logically distinct forms of knowledge, each with its own methods of inquiry, its own defined subject-matter and conceptual structure, its own forms of argument and justification. They represent the accepted means by which students are able to make sense of the world, to contribute towards the solution of its problems, and to advance human understanding. Even if it has to be acknowledged – so the argument runs – that real-life issues do not divide neatly into categories susceptible of treatment by one discipline alone, there is no other valid way in which questions can be posed, investigated and answered than in terms of the various academic specialisms which have evolved and developed over the years.

Barriers between different pupil abilities and interests

The third main form of curricular fragmentation is that caused by individual differences among the pupils themselves. Fierce and bitter ideological battles are waged between those who hold that all are born more or less equal, but have differences imposed upon them by their upbringing and their environment, and their rivals who contend that all are born different and unequal according to their ancestry. Both, however, admit that children, by the time they come to primary school, and most certainly by the time they reach secondary school, do in fact display a very diverse range of interests and talents.

Moreover, the less narrow-minded advocates of the 'nature is all' doctrine may be prepared to admit that biological determinism is not so remorseless as to deny any scope at all for education to improve on natural endowment. Indeed, they can be among the most vocal in their insistence on maintaining educational standards – an insistence which would be pointless if schooling had no power to enhance 'innate ability'.

The less blinkered adherents of the 'nurture is all' doctrine may be equally prepared to admit that sociological determinism is not so powerful as to be uniquely accountable for the musical genius of a Mozart and the simple-mindedness of one who is mentally handicapped; they may also concede that, however important environmental factors might be, the school itself can have only a relatively marginal influence in relation to that exercised by the home and the peer group.

Far below the cloudy heights where this Olympian tourney continues to be joined, teachers who differ from one another in a whole variety of ways contend with pupils who also differ from one another in a whole variety of ways. The problem is not to account for, and not necessarily even to minimize, the differences; it is to cope with them. And every attempt to cope very soon leads into a whole range of political issues, to which the nature–nurture controversy is itself largely irrelevant (though its different implicit value-stances may be reflected in the different proposed solutions).

Traditional forms of school organization embody one fairly obvious way of responding to diversity – or at least diverse levels of academic competence. A heterogeneous population can, in terms of this approach, be sifted first into broad 'ability bands'. The categories are familiar enough: the abnormally intelligent, the reasonably bright, the moderately able, the relatively slow and the educationally subnormal. In many educational systems, the sifting takes place by means of an organized assessment procedure or formal test (the much-disliked 'eleven-plus' in England is only one instance), and two or more different types of secondary school house the graded results. Within these different schools – themselves implicitly labelled as providing for first- or second-class citizens, as the case might be – the pupils are often more finely graded, either into 'streams' according to their overall academic performance or into 'sets' which reflect their differing competences in different subject areas. In extreme form, this assumes that, at the end of the process of classification, the resulting groups of pupils are to all intents and purposes homogeneous in ability, and can therefore be taught as efficiently as if they were a single individual: as long as the teacher is skilful enough to pitch his or her message at the right frequency, it will be picked up by every receiver to which it is directed.

Critics argue that a once-for-all allocation to either an 'academic' or a 'non-academic' school at the beginning of the secondary stage is arbitrary and unfair, since it can be shown that a given individual's performance varies over time (so that a score at the age of eleven of, say, 95 on a test with a 'normal quotient' of 100 may well rise or fall by five points or more a couple of years later). In so far as the sorting process works at all, they maintain, it does so by setting up a self-fulfilling prophecy. Every child singled out for membership of the élite group continues to be reminded in a host of subtle ways that he or she is clever; and all children not so singled out have it similarly drummed into them that they are dull. Both groups tend to live up, or down, to expectations.

Can children in any case be sorted according to a test based on a one-dimensional notion of human ability? Typically, the test (or sometimes a relatively small battery of tests) purports to calibrate, in apparently precise numerical terms, individual scores along a single linear scale. Thus, it appears possible to say of this pupil that he or she has, say, twelve more units of 'intelligence', 'ability' or whatever than that one. But expressed in this form, the implausibility of the enterprise becomes obvious. All of us know from experience that individuals differ not along one dimension but many; that the capacity to profit from and enjoy schooling is dependent on a varied combination of different characteristics, and not on any single one. Any attempt to reduce this complexity to the level of one handy and administratively convenient measurement is as absurd as trying to paint somebody's portrait on a length of string.

This diversity of interests, abilities and concerns will continue to exist among children even within a group selected for its likeness in one respect. Yet the allocation system in its very nature encourages teachers to think of them as more or less identical, at least for peda-gogic purposes: it imposes a crudity of perception which must surely jeopardize the complex and delicate process of teaching and learning. (On this line of reasoning, deliberately heterogeneous groupings are to be preferred, at least in serving as a constant reminder to teachers that their pupils are individuals and need to be treated as such.)

There is now a fair amount of evidence also to suggest that testing procedures, however technically ingenious, remain stubbornly context-dependent: the milieu in which the pupil lives strongly conditions his or her test performance. Thus a pupil with a deprived home background in a socially run-down neighbourhood is almost automatically penalized in comparison with a peer from a 'good' home in a culturally and economically rich area. Social reformers, then, have often led the pressure against this system of selection (as a result of which many European countries have now abandoned it): arguing that socially deprived children should not be isolated in ghetto schools and labelled academic failures, but should instead be offered not merely equal but qualitatively better facilities – that schools ought to compensate for the deficiencies of the rest of society.

Apart from being educationally inefficient and socially divisive, traditional forms of secondary school organization have been attacked on grounds more obviously and directly relevant to the theme of this chapter. The different categories of secondary school (the 'academic', the 'vocational', and – in those systems which celebrate the distinction – the 'technical') each have distinctly different forms of curriculum. Thus, the members of the academic élite have a strong diet comprising separate discipline-based components – a mildly diluted, and rather more broadly based, version of the provision which they are expected later to encounter at university. Their less favoured peers are nearly always nourished with more pulpy fare, carefully and considerately designed for those with feebler powers of digestion. There is a greater emphasis on 'practical activities' (the assumption presumably being that this befits future manual workers) and on the 'relevance' of the curriculum to the world outside; much less concern with specialized academic subjects and much more with the basic skills of literacy and numeracy. Thus curricular differences are institutionalized and used to reinforce the existing social divisions.

In attacking the iniquities of such a situation, the exponents of comprehensive education move quickly on to the offensive. Instead of institutionalizing class barriers, why should not the schools be positively concerned with breaking them down? In extreme form this might involve arguing for a romantic ideal in which *all* pupils should be exposed to the high academic culture which is their birthright, irrespective of their academic ability, while at the same time insisting that all pupils must learn to be clever with their hands as well as their heads. At a more modest level, there is widespread support for the compromise view that both traditions should be combined within the framework of a single curriculum.

But, as an answer to the potentially divisive nature of secondary education, the comprehensive school – based on the American 'all through' high school – leaves open many basic questions. It may be large enough to serve all the educational needs of an area, and be staffed and equipped to cope with pupils of all levels of ability. But a sudden enforced merger of élite with non-élite schools (sometimes in a glossily new and expensive building, but sometimes on the basis of their existing premises on separate sites) is probably not a necessary, and certainly not a sufficient, means by which to 'democratize' and unify the curriculum. The crucial change is rather that of attitude and perspective among secondary teachers. Sometimes it seems as if the only distinction between a 'streamed' or 'setted' comprehensive on the one hand, and a grammar school and secondary modern existing side by side on the other, is that the former is much larger and less personal. But a change of emphasis from grouping pupils according to their *ability* (however measured) to attempting to provide for them according to their *interests* (however identified) can have profound curricular implications.

There is a natural tendency to tackle the issue, as many English schools have done, by building up as wide a range of options among different course offerings, from the age of thirteen or fourteen onwards, as the combined resources of the staff will allow. Few schools are ready in practice to sanction a completely *à la carte* choice, particularly in the earlier years: notions of a properly balanced educational diet die hard. But within the broad area of, say, science, pupils might have a choice between more 'academic' courses in physics, chemistry and biology and more 'relevant' courses on science in society, elementary electronics or home economics. Similarly, within the humanities there might be traditional courses (geared to the Ordinary Level examinations) in history and English literature, alongside courses worked out on a more thematic basis and geared to such contemporary issues as living in cities, the problems of minority groups, or family life.

However, the schools which have approached the problem along these lines have encountered various practical difficulties. The first is that unless the school is very large (certainly more than 1500 pupils) the actual choice available to pupils must necessarily be restricted – there simply are not the staff available to meet all the potential requirements. The second is that the wider the range of options, the more difficult it will be for every pupil to make a sensible choice among them: and this creates a subsidiary need for strong tutorial and counselling support. What with the demands on staff time for this additional guidance, and the fact that some options will inevitably attract fewer pupils and so be uneconomic to run, the *à la carte* curriculum can begin to look unattractive on economic grounds. But it is also open to a more fundamental objection. Certain courses, especially those for pupils within the fourteen-to-sixteen age range, are likely to be designed to lead to some external examinations; others will not be so designed. Inevitably, the pupils will begin to identify themselves as academic or non-academic, even if the teachers advising them have not already done so; and before long, there will be seen to be one set of curriculum options for the bright and another for the dull. At this point, the distinction between such an arrangement and the one it was designed to replace begins to look more apparent than real.

Another approach manages to avoid most of the difficulties of the *à la carte* options system, though it gives rise to problems of its own. It is based on the notion of a 'common-core curriculum' to be followed by *all* secondary school pupils, regardless of whether or not they are destined for subsequent academic careers, and regardless of what their current concerns might happen to be. The common-core curriculum has obvious attractions as a democratic device: it seems to hold promise of providing all children, regardless of social environment or genetic endowment, with a common stock of knowledge and a shared tradition of values and understandings. And, of course, once this core has been identified, the rest of the curriculum can be built up round it according to the local circumstances of the school and the individual interests of its pupils.

But therein lies the rub. A series of articles by both practising teachers and curriculum theorists on the nature of the core curriculum was published in *The Times Educational Supplement* during 1975.[3] The lesson which it perhaps brought home most clearly was how intimately curricular decisions are related to value questions, and thus how difficult it is to achieve any form of consensus in a pluralistic culture. There were at least three areas of disagreement among those who contributed to the debate.

The first concerned how large the core should be in relation to the rest of the fruit; the disagreement related to both height and circumference. Some contended that the primary stage of education already furnished a good deal of commonly shared material, and that continuing uniformity would fail to take proper account of the growing diversity of interests of the students themselves: to postpone curricular differentiation beyond the age of, say, fourteen was therefore both unnecessary and undesirable. Others saw this as a mere device to reintroduce selection by academic ability (and hence, indirectly, by social background) at a slightly later age, and were therefore inclined to insist on a common curriculum being marked out until at least sixteen. Again, some felt that the core should be a fairly thin one, embodying no more than the minimum of knowledge and skills needed to enable school leavers to cope adequately in contemporary society, and leaving the major part of the timetable free for pupils to follow their individual interests, as far as the available options allowed. Their opponents saw this as reopening the possibility of one curriculum for the clever and another for the rest, and renewed their insistence that the schools should make a broadly-based common culture accessible to all.

In the second arena for debate, the dispute concentrated on who was to define the common core. Was it to be some central agency, such as the Secretary of State or the Schools Council; or was it to be left to each school to decide? Here the conventional political camps of the right and the left were divided among themselves. It was not merely the extremist advocates of *laissez-faire* who acknowledged the strength (and the virtues) of the decentralized educational tradition of England and Wales; nor was it merely the most dedicated social engineers who maintained that fundamental curricular issues were too important to be left to the teachers. In a sense, the issue had been settled by default. The only obvious central agency, the Schools Council, had in 1971 set up a working party on 'The Whole Curriculum': its report – perhaps wisely – made no attempt to define the content of the aims of secondary education as a whole.[4] Instead, it concentrated on setting out the terms of a suggested 'educational covenant' (to which we shall return in Chapter 10) and offering general guidelines to schools on curriculum design, development and planning. Since neither Parliament nor the Department of Education and Science seemed likely to take up the challenge of setting out the detailed terms of a common secondary curriculum, the status quo was happily preserved. The schools continued to enjoy the myth of individual autonomy within the reality of a whole set of implicit and explicit constraints.

The third set of issues raised during the 'common curriculum' controversy in *The Times Educational Supplement* related to the nature and constitution of the core. On the one side, Dr Rhodes Boyson spelled out a fairly predictable roll-call of items:

About 15 per cent of the week should be spent on English grammar, including parts of speech and the make-up of a sentence. . . . About 100 texts in literature should be laid down of which it would be expected that every pupil covered some 40 books and plays. . . . In geography a thorough grasp of British geography and an in-depth look at Europe should be linked with a basic knowledge of the continents and the major countries . . . a strong case can be made for the teaching of perspective and colour in art and joints and materials in wood-work . . .

On the other side, Dr Eric Midwinter pinned his hopes on the mastery of functional skills rather than the assimilation of knowledge, listing some of the aspects of adult life with which students had to come to terms: 'Human relations . . .; the consumer nature of the economy . . .; the civic structure of their community . . .; the leisure opportunities of their daily lives . . .'; and so on.

The distinction between education as facts to be learnt and education as skills to be developed is not as sharp as those who wish to use it for logic-chopping purposes are prone to make out. Most knowledge entails some skill, if only an ability to differentiate one thing from another; and many skills demand some prerequisite knowledge. But in whichever terms one defines the desiderata, their selection still depends on individual taste – the number of things which it can be claimed, more or less reasonably, that every school-leaver should know is far, far in excess of what it is reasonable to expect every school-leaver to have learnt.

It is the sheer relativism of curriculum-building, in a society which allows few absolutes, that is likely to bring to an end the argument about a common core. Of course there are a few things on which almost everybody would agree, such as the need to learn to read and write. These obvious points of agreement are already firmly built into both the primary and secondary curriculum; a core confined merely to them would seem slim to the point of emaciation. But there are many other things on which some people would agree and others would not. To get round this problem, some educational systems have set up central agencies to make the fairly arbitrary choice of what the common core shall comprise, while others allow the individual schools (or, as in the USA, the individual school boards) to hammer out the necessary compromises for themselves. Such decentralized decision-making leads, more often than not, to a *post hoc* general consensus shaped less by logic than by some pragmatic combination of external examination requirements; the availability of textbooks, classroom materials and suitably trained teachers; and the prevailing educational climate. It is as elusive to track down – but as obvious to observe – as the consensus at any given time on what paperbacks to read, what clothes to wear and what music to listen to.

All this suggests that any definitive, once-for-all attempt to settle the common-core curriculum is doomed to failure. But, as we argued in Chapter 1, the curriculum needs to be interpreted in a much wider sense than simply its subject-matter or its goals; it could well be that its successful integration depends less on the commonality of its required knowledge or skills than on the coherence of its approach and on the cohesion of its organizing framework.

Some integrating strategies

We have mentioned the concern of social reformers to find ways of using schooling to compensate for social disadvantage, and thus by exercising 'positive discrimination' to give as many pupils as possible the educational privileges which were once reserved for the élite minority. Trial and error have shown that genuine reform is to be achieved neither by tinkering with the external structure of the system nor by modifying its internal structure. That is to say, simply sending all the children in an area to one very large secondary school in the place of several smaller ones of itself achieves nothing; and simply drawing up a new common syllabus seems to achieve relatively little either. What emerges as central to the notion of comprehensive reform is that all pupils should be encouraged to see themselves, in at least some respect, as successes rather than failures; and that they should be given at least initial access to all the main areas of intellectual understanding.

In his Penguin, *Resources for Learning*, L. C. Taylor argues that a genuinely comprehensive school must necessarily base its instruction on materials rather than on the teacher.[5] An essential consequence of 'going comprehensive' is that every class deliberately blends pupils with different home backgrounds, different degrees of academic competence and different interests. Every pupil has then to be treated as an individual; the emphasis must be switched from teaching to learning so that members of the class are enabled for most of the time to work individually and in small groups on suitably organized tasks. The most convenient way to organize these tasks is through appropriate resource materials – booklets, question sheets, work cards, anthologies of texts for group discussion, audio-tapes and the like – with the teacher acting as manager, consultant and tutor as the need arises.

Such a pattern of classroom organization has long been established in the progressive English primary schools. Secondary schools, though, have to meet a more complex set of curricular demands, and at the same time to sustain the professional confidence of their discipline-based specialist teachers. Yet to avoid excessive (and probably needless) specialization in the early stages of the secondary schools, and allow pupils the longer time-spans which resource-based learning demands, something positive has to be done to reduce the number of separate subject components in the timetable.

A reassuringly straightforward answer has found favour in a sizeable number of comprehensive schools. One of its earliest proponents was Countesthorpe College, which forms perhaps the most thoroughgoing and widely publicized attempt to work out a new rationale for a British comprehensive school – and whose founder, Tim McMullen, was co-director with L. C. Taylor of the Nuffield Resources for Learning Project in the late 1960s.[6]

Countesthorpe is atypical in many respects: it was not only purpose-built, but – because its first head teacher (styled Warden) was able to choose his own staff – it developed from the outset a distinctive and coherent style and approach. Its internal governance is highly democratic: decisions are made by consensus among all the staff and representatives of the students, rather than simply by the head or his senior teachers. But it has also created a curricular pattern which provides an interesting blend of interdisciplinarity with individual and small-group learning: and it is this point which is directly relevant here.

At Countesthorpe, and in other schools which have adopted a similar pattern, the traditional disciplines are grouped into three or four broadly based areas of inquiry. The exact constitution of each cluster may vary slightly according to taste (mathematics, for example, though it might usually be classed with the sciences, could possibly be bracketed with 'forms of communication'); so may the defining features of the clusters themselves. But, by and large, the pattern is to link humanities subjects (e.g. English literature, history, religious education and human geography) in one group; languages (including the development of English language skills) in another; the sciences in a third; and practical and creative arts in a fourth. Time is then allocated on the timetable to these interdisciplinary areas rather than to individual subjects, and the teachers in each group are encouraged to work out introductory courses which draw upon all the constituent disciplines but do not prematurely differentiate between them. This is a good deal easier said than done; but three different strategies, each relating to a particular aspect of interdisciplinarity, have been adapted from primary school and university experience to help cope with the problem, and are gradually edging their way into the comprehensive classroom.

The first is to organize the teachers themselves into a close-knit team, under a team chairman, to formulate course outlines, write and assemble background materials, and where necessary give joint presentations or take part jointly in seminar discussions. The second is to build up course content around issues of major current concern – the problems of racial prejudice, say, or threats to the environment – in the hope both of arousing the pupils' interest and of helping them to appreciate the differing contributions which different disciplines can make to the understanding of such issues. The third is to encourage the pupils to work through collective discussion and collaborative inquiry, as well as through individual projects, so as to help ensure that they are actively engaged in intellectual exploration.[7]

How far a curriculum integrated along these lines can meet the needs of comprehensive education is not easy to judge. The movement away from premature subject specialization is widely supported, but the powers of resistance of established disciplines are far from negligible. Indeed, as far as large-scale curriculum development is concerned, the scene in most countries has been dominated by subject-based projects. It is to a consideration of how the results of such projects can be put into practice and evaluated that we now turn.

8 Responsiveness to change

New ideas, in education as in life, travel hopefully: few of them actually arrive at their intended destinations.[1] So it is not altogether surprising to find a recent writer on curricular innovation complaining that 'For nearly two decades now, we have seen large amounts of capital invested in the production of a variety of new curricula . . . much of this effort has had relatively little impact on the daily routine of the average classroom teacher.'[2]

Perhaps because of their evolutionary and haphazard nature, the traditional processes of curriculum development did not recognize a need for any carefully coordinated strategy to promulgate the new ideas they generated. But it seems curious in retrospect that the pioneers of the heuristic movement did not foresee that each major phase of development would need an equally sustained effort to ensure that its results could be put into effective practice. It is true that what was described in Chapter 5 as the 'research, development and diffusion' model pays lip-service to the idea of 'delivering the completed product' to the schools for whom it is intended; and that the 'social-interaction' and 'problem-solving' models have acknowledged the existence of the problem in their different ways. Nevertheless, most of those involved in the business of curriculum change would admit that, while a good deal is now known about how to plan, construct and try out new curriculum schemes, no one has yet come up with a sensible way of weaving such schemes into the daily fabric of classroom life.

This chapter attempts to explore some of the issues of dissemination from the point of view of the sponsoring agency and the development team. The teachers and pupils at the receiving end have, of course, a very different perspective; and one which, we would argue, is even more important when it comes to assessing the success or failure of curricular innovation in the long run. We shall consider the acceptability of change from their standpoint later on, in Chapter 10.

Recognizing the need for dissemination

The spreading of new ideas and practices has been given a variety of labels. The two words which appear to be in most common currency are diffusion and dissemination – and perhaps the neatest way of contrasting them is one suggested by Peter Kelly: dissemination is what the curriculum developer intends to happen; diffusion is what happens in practice. Or to put the point less finely, dissemination denotes some sort of conscious, systematic strategy for promulgating new ideas, while diffusion refers to the actual process of their promulgation. As we have already remarked, the latter is ineffective in the case of curriculum development when the former has been ignored.

Attempts to analyse, as opposed to define, the concept of dissemination invariably highlight the methodological bias of the analyst. For example, it is impossible to miss the technocratic overtones of the RD and D model in this prescription by Clark and Hopkins:[3] 'Inform target systems; demonstrate solutions and programmes; train target system in use of solutions and programmes; service and nurture installed solution.' Nor does one need exceptional hearing to catch the echoes of social interaction in the alternative formulation by Katz, Lewin and Hamilton:[4] 'Acceptance, over time, of some specific item, idea or practice, by individuals, groups or other adopting units, linked by specific channels of communication to a social structure and to a given system of values and culture.' Indeed, the underlying ideology of the development process infects all its activities. Thus dissemination of an RD-and-D-based development programme attracts military metaphors: the talk, the thinking behind it, and the way it is carried out centre on 'strategies', 'delivery systems' and the like. Similarly (as we shall go on to argue in more detail in Chapter 9), the choice of evaluators for a particular project, and the style in which they conduct their task, tend to accord with, rather than conflict with, that project's underlying assumptions.

But definition, analysis and the formulation of hypotheses are not our main purpose here. We shall try rather 'to understand the difficulties of making new ideas and approaches accessible'; and consider how 'to ensure that investments in innovation actually influence the system and are not building private wisdoms among those involved in planning and development'.[5] The first step in tackling these twin tasks is to consider why, in the early days of the heuristic movement, curriculum developers concentrated on the planning, production, trial and revision of new curricular offerings to the exclusion of their dissemination. The simple answer is that dissemination was not seen as a major problem. The developers assumed that, once the wraps had been taken off any thoroughly tested and well-designed set of materials, once they came on the market for all to buy, the rest could be left to the good sense and sound judgement of the intended consumers.

It took some years before this assumption was seen to be false. At first, cheering references were made to the inevitable time that was needed for new ideas to be assimilated – research evidence was produced to show that the dissemination of any innovation followed a recognizable S-curve, with a modest initial growth leading to a period of rapid expansion and gradually tailing off again to account for the 'slow adopters'. Later, as the disappointing results of 'usage surveys' began to come in, there was much talk of the innate conservatism of the teaching profession. The intended consumers, it seemed, were surprisingly short on both good sense and sound judgement. The real explanations only emerged long afterwards – that teaching materials alone cannot carry the weight of much traffic in innovative ideas; and that any proposals are foredoomed which assume all schools to be identical.

In Chapter 5 we indicated how the realization of this led developers to acknowledge that not only must local circumstances be taken into account but that any major development programme must be complemented by an equally ambitious effort to communicate its philosophy to teachers, to show them how to put it into practice, and to help them modify it to fit their own context.

Other factors retarded efforts at dissemination. Most sponsors of development work were understandably reluctant to appear to be undermining the professional autonomy of teachers. Fund-giving agencies are commonly debarred, by tradition if not by law, from going beyond backing the development of new ideas to the quasi-political process of advancing a particular cause. The danger of distorting the free trade in ideas by attaching too heavy a subsidy to any one of them is as great in education as elsewhere; most people involved in it would rather see curricular decisions made in the untidy market-place of democracy than have them neatly imposed by the prestige or the power of a wealthy patron.

In avoiding this real danger the early sponsors of heuristic curriculum programmes failed to draw an important distinction. It lies between conveying information about a new set of ideas adequately enough to help teachers make their own informed judgements on whether or not to take them up, and proselytizing a particular cause in a way that amounts to unfair propaganda or a subtle attempt to brainwash.

With the passing of time, curriculum sponsors overcame their reluctance to support dissemination as well as development. The two main funding agencies in England and Wales have each shown, in their different ways, a growing concern to help the spread of new curricular ideas. The Nuffield Foundation had decided, even before the first of the Nuffield project publications came on the market, to set aside a sizeable proportion of the proceeds from sales towards 'after-care' activities. As a result of this decision, experiments could be made with a variety of different dissemination approaches and a diverse range of courses for teachers. The Schools Council took a more cautious line, deciding not to fund project dissemination automatically but to consider each proposal on its merits. It set up a working party to review the problem, and this produced a useful, if rather dull, report.[6] It has recently begun to give greater emphasis, and more generous funding, to the follow-up work consequent on any new development scheme; though its activities are limited by the proscription from trespassing on the territory of the already established agencies for in-service training.

A further reason for the relative neglect of dissemination is the brief, butterfly life of most curriculum development teams. Because development agencies prefer to fund specific short-term projects rather than more general long-term ones, they tend to recruit teams to work at a particular task for three or four years only, and thereafter to maintain only a kind of skeleton crew for basic maintenance. Even when sponsors try, as they now seem to be doing, to adopt a more flexible approach and to get away from the project mentality, other problems arise. Surprisingly often, those entrusted with the main responsibility for dissemination – say a chosen team of local authority advisers, a group of teachers' centre wardens, or the staff of one or more colleges of education – have had very little to do with the original development, and may not adequately understand the intentions of its authors. The difficulties of devising a workable formula still seems a long way from resolution. Before we analyse the likely needs, however, it may be useful to consider what actually happens when an innovative idea comes into currency.

Taking up ideas

Motives for taking up new ideas may be mixed. In education – as in any enterprise which depends more on the uncertainty of human interplay than on the assurance of science – fashion is one factor. As Michael Frayn wrote in the *Observer* (18 June 1967):

> The way the dissemination of ideas works around our way is that first my good friend Christopher Crumble gets to hear about them, and makes me feel insecure. Then I catch up and make Horace Morris feel insecure. By the time Horace had discovered the meaning and omnipresence of charisma, for example, I was right off it – no one seemed charismatic to me any more . . . I was on to 'symbiosis' – and Christopher Crumble, the Speedy Gonzales of the intellect, was already out of 'symbiosis' and into 'I–thou' or even 'freakout'.

Many of those who first embrace a new idea are the lively, enthusiastic and imaginative teachers who are quick to see the possibilities it offers for improving their own teaching; but some may simply have a vague dissatisfaction with the status quo, or believe that 'getting in on the act' will improve their standing or career prospects. Many of those most resistant to change are the sincere and dedicated teachers who are rightly suspicious of gimmicks or cure-alls, and who are anxious to safeguard the long-term interests of their pupils; but others are merely dull, unimaginative, or too lazy to alter their established routines. It is much too simplistic to equate 'innovative' with 'good' or 'conservative' with 'bad' (or, of course, vice versa).

Whatever the motives for responding to an innovative idea may be, the consequences of that response tend to follow a familiar pattern. The initial enthusiasm is usually over-generous. Hopes run high that here, at last, lies revealed the solution to many – if not all – of one's problems: everything that is proposed is uncritically embraced.

But once theory has to be put into practice, all sorts of hidden snags begin to reveal themselves. Those who have never understood the new idea in the first place, or who have only invested in it in a fit of fancy, tend to give up at this stage – and perhaps the while to complain that they have been cheated. Its more serious disciples either discover that they have misinterpreted the intentions behind it, and modify their practice accordingly; or realize that, in order to make it work in their particular situation, they must necessarily adapt it in certain important ways. In very few cases does the original idea, as first interpreted by its recipients, survive unchanged.

Three consequences would seem to follow. The first is that un-critical espousal of any new scheme must be tempered. Curriculum developers, in their understandable anxiety to present their wares in the best light, tend to over-sell them, to much the same extent as responding teachers tend to over-buy. The resulting inflation of demand and expectancy is of eventual benefit to neither.

The second consequence is that teachers need an opportunity, once they are adequately informed about the nature and aims of a given curriculum programme, to come to terms with the changes in perspective and approach which it implies. Attendance at a suitable course may well help them to understand more fully how the subject-matter is to be interpreted, and how the relationships between pupils and teachers are likely to be affected. Some teachers will be able to learn the necessary skills and adjust their attitudes without any special help; others may prefer, instead of attending a course, to to spend a day talking to someone closely familiar with the project in question, or visiting a school where the new programme is already successfully under way.

The third point concerns the difficulties which emerge at the critical juncture when innovative ideas are first put to test in the classroom. Even the most experienced of teachers may find them-selves at sea when faced with an unfamiliar mass of material which is meant to be presented in an unfamiliar way to pupils who are equally unused to the change in circumstances. The well-tried strategies for adjusting the syllabus and finding the methods to suit the collective idiosyncrasies of this year's Form 4C will often fail to work under the new dispensation. Other means have to be devised of adapting the unconventional image to fit the conventional situation. It is at this moment that the teacher involved with a new development may be most in need of support; and the agency concerned with promul-gating that development will certainly be falling down on its job if it fails to provide it.

It seems, then, that there are at least three main components in any realistic attempt to disseminate the results of a curriculum programme. They might be labelled, respectively, consumer com-munication, teacher education and classroom support. It may be useful now to unpack each of the parcels to which these labels are attached, and to look briefly at their contents.

Consumer communication

Marshall McLuhan has given universal currency to the idea that communication consists of a message and a medium, and that the two are closely interconnected. Like most elegant simplifications, this leaves aside certain important factors, such as the nature of the audience and the context within which the message is purveyed. But certainly the way in which an educational development is communicated to its potential audience in the schools does affect the content of what is received.

The more complex and all-embracing the innovative idea, the more it requires full explanation and fair presentation. Such crude slogans as 'the integrated day', 'team teaching', 'discovery methods' or the 'Dalton plan' may have usefully stimulated the imagination and energy of teachers, but the schools which took these as a shared rallying-cry put on them as varied interpretations as the schools themselves were varied. Again, when 'open-plan schooling' was all the rage, the main thing which its practitioners had in common – amid an astonishingly diverse set of activities and procedures – was their staunch conviction that each was running an open-plan school in the full and true sense of the phrase.

If developers are concerned to avoid wasting the time, thought and effort they have put into working out and elaborating a programme, testing it and assessing its real possibilities, they need also to ensure that their work is understood. Otherwise the potential beneficiaries, the pupils themselves, may have to make do with a heavily despoiled residue of their intended inheritance.

We referred earlier to the haziness of the boundary which divides information from propaganda, and to the dangers as well as the temptations which beset the curriculum developer in exaggerating his claims. Early dissemination attempts tended to display only the best features of a new programme and play down the potential snags, not necessarily in order to deceive, but because it seemed inconvenient and inappropriate to bring them deliberately to view. But in recent years numerous projects have taken a more mature and responsible attitude towards their clientele, recognizing that the central purpose of dissemination is to give teachers a fuller opportunity to exercise their professional judgement according to their own needs, rather than to coax them into accepting a pre-ordained solution to their problems. A curriculum team has to direct the information it offers towards helping schools to make wise decisions about whether to adopt a new programme, on what basis and with what end in view. For example, the first of the Nuffield science projects (on O Level physics) was at pains to stress that its offerings were designed specifically for the most able students and that it would be both difficult and costly to implement. Again, the Nuffield Primary French team attempted seriously – though often vainly – to urge schools not to adopt their programme without both a well-qualified teacher and a guarantee from the secondary schools who took their pupils that the learning sequence would be continued at the appropriate stage. But perhaps the most sophisticated example of the new style of communication (as of many other aspects of the curriculum development process) was provided by the Humanities Curriculum Project.[7]

The development team, helped by the Project's evaluation staff, devoted a considerable part of their effort to observing how different trial schools managed to cope with the problems of putting the new scheme into effect. They produced videotapes, audiotapes and transcripts of samples of classroom activity; and they prepared case studies of the various ways in which the power politics of the school and the local authority could help or hinder successful implementation. They used this material as the basis for a more open diagloue with those interested in adopting the programme when it was completed. They tried to emphasize that what was involved was not a simple matter of following set instructions in a teacher's handbook, but a complex and demanding business of interpreting shared intentions in a whole diversity of situations, and under a wide but unpredictable range of constraints. In this, they may have been ahead of their time. The teachers and the local authorities, unused to full frontal exposure, were shocked and puzzled: it was even suspected that the Project was playing a cunning double game, apparently discouraging potential customers the more to whet their appetites for joining an exclusive club. But now that the consumers themselves have had a taste of the truth, many have come to prefer it to bland and misleading assurances. Future programmes are likely to offer richer as well as more extensive information than in the past, so that potential users are better able to decide whether or not to take up the innovative challenge and to cope with the consequences of doing so.

If the nature of the message has begun to change, so have the ways it is communicated. Organizing dissemination meetings on a regional or local basis has become a fairly standard practice. Personal contact, even for as little as an evening, or a morning or afternoon, between one of the development team (or a teacher involved in the early trials) and the prospective clientele seems the only way to provide a genuine opportunity to ask questions as well as to be told about the aims and intentions of the programme. One good way of giving the flavour of a curriculum programme is to show it in action. A real teacher with real pupils brings the developers' intentions alive in a way that words on a page, however well composed, or conference speeches, however eloquent, cannot. So any meeting of teachers and local authority officials organized to introduce a new scheme will now tend to expect films and videotapes of classroom activity as a standard part of the provision. In addition, many projects produce special 'sample kits' showing the style and coverage of the published materials, together with a variety of handouts which interested teachers can take home and study at their leisure.

Other, more well-established communication routes still remain open, and are still used. The national Inspectorate and the local authority advisers continue to alert the schools they visit to new developments, and for that reason are themselves eagerly wooed by curriculum agencies. The publishers of project materials are another interested party, and will often reinforce the team's efforts by drawing on their own range of contacts. In major conferences where a slot in the programme is given to a particular scheme, the publisher concerned will usually take the opportunity to exhibit the whole range of its publications and perhaps to demonstrate some visual materials as well. One useful means of transmission of new educational ideas is through the professional teacher associations. In some countries these associations have a large membership of specialist teachers in a given subject field, and enjoy considerable prestige among teachers in both universities and schools; their voice is respected by education ministers and ministry and local authority officials. They usually issue regular journals as well as occasional monographs, and organize annual conferences on a national and a regional basis. Perhaps because of their close identification with the establishment, they tend to be cautious about espousing apparently revolutionary curricular causes, but if a curriculum sponsor can manage to gain their sympathy, his task of communication becomes a great deal easier. (There are indeed cases where, as we saw in Chapter 5, such associations have themselves played an active part in initiating subject-based innovation.)

In recent years, the educational press, too, has become a force to be reckoned with. Although it cannot, of course, shape teacher opinion as strongly for or against a particular innovation as can the professional bodies or the Inspectorate, it provides a quick and pervasive means of attracting teachers' attention, as well as a useful forum for public debate. Many project directors have found that it pays good dividends to keep educational journalists in touch with the progress of their teams' work and to write periodic articles describing their aims and achievements.

The main obstacle which prevents information getting through to those teachers for whom it may be relevant is not the lack of means but the sheer numbers of those who need to know. The largest torrent, once it is spilled out in many directions at once, loses its force. But this difficulty, serious though it seems, can be a strong incentive for the development teams to think carefully about what they are trying to do. They may begin to ask themselves fundamental questions about whether they want to sell a particular package or to advocate certain general principles; to encourage conformity or promote individual initiative among teachers. They may also begin to analyse the differing needs of their different audiences – does a local adviser or teachers' centre warden need the same evidence to judge whether a particular scheme should be recommended or not as a head teacher does to decide whether to approve its adoption in his school?

To make sure that the potential audience is prepared to listen is another matter. Whether or not the climate of opinion in a particular school, or a particular local authority, or an education system as a whole, is such that those who work within it will be receptive to a given set of ideas cannot always be predicted, and certainly cannot be controlled. Of course, the trials of any new development will offer some clues; but all sorts of factors may inhibit successful communication. An innovation which represents a significant departure from common practice, or demands apparently complicated technical facilities, may daunt many teachers. If it seems that the average pupils in a school cannot cope with it, teachers may dismiss it on educational grounds. If it requires the special provision of small classes or of expensive apparatus, heads and administrators may rule it out as too costly. And so on. It is little wonder that many schemes have succeeded more notably in generating innovative ideas than in disseminating them. But although the communication problem remains unsolved, there is no scarcity of new projects prepared to tackle it: and the state of the art is already a good deal further advanced than it was ten years ago.

Teacher education

In-service teacher training is a longer-established notion than that of heuristic curriculum development. It traditionally takes the form of a range of optional courses lasting anything from a day to a week, organized by a variety of different agencies, and often taking place in the school holidays. Great as is the potential of this instrument of traditional development, it has in most countries only marginally contributed towards improving the quality of education.

The first reason is that its function is often perceived as 'training' in a fairly narrow sense: as instructing teachers in the use of new techniques or as informing them about new subject-matter in their specialist fields. It is seldom seen as an opportunity for providing *education permanente*; or as a chance to enable the educators themselves to re-think their ideas or to experiment with new approaches.[8] Secondly, because its provision is usually *laissez-faire* and totally uncoordinated, its coverage tends to be patchy and sporadic; and since there is in most systems no powerful in-service agency pressing for an adequate share of the total educational budget, the resources allotted are marginal, and liable to drastic cuts in times of economic scarcity. Thirdly, because participation is voluntary, the teachers who are keen enough to attend courses are usually those least in need of support; those who are pathetic or unwilling to expose their incompetence have no incentive to change their ways. This absurdity is reinforced if, as often happens, teachers have to meet part of the costs of attendance and tuition out of their own pockets. (Things are ordered differently in the USA, where teachers are salaried for only ten months in the year, and where those attending summer courses are paid to do so. But this results, inevitably, in some teachers collecting courses as if they were postage stamps.) Fourth, because the majority of courses are short, they can make only a minor impact; because they usually involve only one teacher at most in a given school, that teacher – even if he returns with new ideas – may have great difficulty in persuading his colleagues to introduce change on a significant scale.

The catalogue of criticisms could, no doubt, be extended further; but, with all its faults, traditional post-experience teacher training has in the past provided the only available organism on to which curriculum projects could graft their own induction courses for interested school staff. In nearly every case, development agencies (which were, as we noted earlier, initially hesitant about tackling the problems of dissemination) either decided against or were precluded from setting up their own structures for teacher education, and relied instead on the available machinery. This being in most countries so ramshackle, the dissemination of new programmes was seriously inhibited.

At the outset, induction programmes for heuristic curriculum projects embodied most of the prevailing assumptions about in-service training. Their characteristic form was that of a Baptist immersion – a quick one-week dip into the new ideology, from which the converts emerged fortified to carry the gospel to all the folks back home. The fact that few managed to establish a thriving mission was put down to the frailties of human nature: the deficiencies of theological technique were not in question.

With the growing awareness that it is important to put curriculum schemes effectively into practice, the situation has begun to change. And of course the changes, because they reflect back on in-service programmes in general, have also helped to shift attitudes and emphases. Courses are increasingly concerned with professional education in the fullest sense. Gradually, the intensive induction has given place to the more sustained attempt, over a term or maybe a year, to involve teachers in reviewing their own efforts to implement a new curriculum. Dialogue has replaced didacticism; and, though it is more prolonged, it has also turned out to be more productive. (This acknowledgement of the professional competence of the teacher has profound implications: we will discuss some of them in Chapter 10.)

Once curriculum developers began to accommodate more to the actual needs of the teacher than to the limited conceptions of the in-service trainer, it became clear that the scope of their activity had to be considerably extended. Since the tactic of selecting a single member of staff to bear the whole burden of introducing a new programme has proved demonstrably futile, attention has turned instead to the context which surrounds the classroom. Teacher education is no longer seen as a matter of singling out an elect few, but as a process of helping a whole institution to review its established routines. This means giving attention to *all* those who are likely to be affected by the introduction of a curricular change – not only the subject department (or departments) directly concerned, but also the head teacher and his more senior and influential colleagues. Indeed, it involves going wider than this, and putting the relevant local authority staff – and particularly the Chief Education Officer and the appropriate specialist adviser – adequately in the picture.

As long as the training programmes associated with a new development project were modelled on the pattern of traditional 'in-service' courses and aimed to bring together for three or four days a hundred or so interested volunteers from schools all over the country, the job of running them could reasonably be tackled by the central project group. But the wider brief outlined above requires other agents to reinforce the effort. The Schools Council Modern Languages Project, for example, built on the experience of the more lively and creative teachers involved in the Project trials. The development team concentrated its own efforts on training the disseminators, and they in turn took on responsibility in their own localities for speaking at regional conferences, running short courses, and in some cases organizing longer-term study groups of colleagues actively concerned to implement the new programme in their schools.

But judged as a long-term strategy for curriculum dissemination, this approach has two main snags. In the first place, its geographical coverage is bound to be patchy. It very seldom happens that a suitable teacher can be found in every region of the country who is able and willing to shoulder the considerable burdens of running a dissemination programme. In the second place, those who are outstanding enough to be singled out as regional project leaders are by the same token those most likely to be promoted to a more responsible post elsewhere; so that the distribution across the country of trained leaders is liable to change drastically in even a relatively short period. Perhaps, therefore, large numbers of trial schools should be taken on so that there is something approaching a nation-wide network of experienced teachers at the outset of the dissemination phase. But the central project team has inevitably to balance this desideratum against the other demands placed on it by its sponsors. Setting up and servicing a school for initial project trials is an expensive and time-consuming business, and few projects have in practice felt able to multiply the numbers into three figures.

Faced with these hazards, one or two projects – the Nuffield Junior Mathematics Project and the Humanities Curriculum Project, for example – have attempted to base their regional activities on institutions rather than on individuals. Even here, of course, there is no one simple formula which can be applied. Local circumstances differ so much that what proves effective in one place – basing a long-term programme on, say, the local university, polytechnic or college of education – may prove disastrous in another. A whole variety of patterns have been tried. In one, a particular school may act as the nucleus for dissemination; in another, it may be a teachers' centre. In others again, an institution is specially created – perhaps an informal but active regional group or (though this has a tendency to become inflexible and ossified) a more formal committee. The main concern of the central development agency must be to ensure that the staff of the relevant group or institution can work as a team – so that if one key individual moves elsewhere, the enterprise can continue unimpeded. Just as the adoption of a new programme demands the commitment of all those affected by it (including the head and the local authority), so too the creation of a local base for dissemination demands that not one but many people must acquire the necessary know-how and must share an enthusiasm and a responsibility for making it more widely available.

Given that effective dissemination has to involve a number of key people in each school, this suggests that the relevant teacher education should take place in the school itself, and should be provided by a local agency. Since the local team will itself usually require prior training, this training too might as well take place in the locality. So the central dissemination group, as well as the local one in its turn, has to be prepared to go round from one place to another, rather than sit at home and call its clients to it. The resulting decentralization of the induction programmes is inevitably less authoritarian in its approach; and because it is rooted in the realities of particular schools, it is likely to take more fully into account their specific possibilities and limitations, and thus to make a given curriculum programme less abstract and more adaptable to the real needs of different institutions.

Classroom support

Even assuming that a curriculum programme has been successful, first in communicating its aims and purposes to its prospective audience, and secondly in helping those who are thinking of adopting it to become more familiar with its detailed workings, a further job remains to be done. Anyone who has tried to acquire a new set of skills – whether it be playing the piano or driving a car – will know the difference between practising under the guidance of an experienced tutor and performing for the first time on one's own in public. Where, perforce, relatively little time can be spent on the initial induction, not only is it difficult to adjust to full independence but all sorts of unforeseen problems may crop up.

As a logical consequence of their taking dissemination more seriously, curriculum developers have also become concerned with the needs of teachers for continuing support after they have decided to adopt a new approach. Of course, a significant number of teachers may be confident enough, or experienced enough, to manage perfectly well on their own. In some cases, the curriculum programme is itself only mildly innovatory, and demands relatively few departures from established practice. In others, those who take it up may so far modify it to fit their own procedures and preconceptions as to make it virtually indistinguishable from what went before. But there nevertheless remain many instances in which major curriculum changes, once introduced into a school, create difficulties which were not anticipated by either the developers themselves or the staff concerned, and which are not easily tackled within the resources of those directly involved.

It was partly to counteract these difficulties that the Nuffield Junior Mathematics Project pioneered the setting up of local teachers' centres. The original idea was that teachers adopting the approach advocated by the curriculum team should be encouraged by their education authorities to come together for regular meetings in a designated 'maths centre'. This, it was argued, would give them the necessary opportunity to discuss, with colleagues who were sharing the same experience, the practical difficulties of implementing the new curriculum and the conceptual difficulties of understanding the (relatively unfamiliar) mathematical ideas which lay behind it. It would also provide an opportunity – for those who wished to take it – to collaborate with staff in other schools in the exacting and time-consuming business of preparing suitable pupils' materials. As we noted in Chapter 5, the Project team had come out firmly against the idea that they should produce such materials, believing that these should be locally based, rooted in the pupils' immediate environment and produced by the teachers themselves. But they were sufficiently realistic to recognize that some teachers would need help from others – help of a kind that local centres might be in a good position to provide.

The idea was generally recognized as a good one, and it quickly caught on. The Schools Council adopted it as part of its general strategy. As new curriculum programmes in subjects other than primary school mathematics reached the point at which their results became generally available, they too urged local authorities to sponsor groups of interested teachers – and understandably enough, the existing mathematics centres were pressed into service to do additional duty for modern languages, English, humanities and the like. Soon, a national network of such centres began to emerge. The system also had its imitators elsewhere. The Netherlands took up on a large scale the idea of teachers' centres as forming an integral part of curriculum development; Germany and the USA have also shown steadily increasing interest.

But intention and execution do not always in practice neatly coincide. Even in the early days, when all that was involved was a local group of teachers with a shared interest in trying out the ideas developed by the Nuffield Junior Mathematics team, a centre in one area could look very different from one in another area. In some cases, special rooms were set aside – often in a recently vacated school building – and generously provided with their own specialist library, various items of equipment, and a full-time warden recruited from one of the local schools. In others, the arrangements were far less ambitious – a classroom or common room in an existing school, designated for use after hours (as if for an evening institute), and staffed by an adviser or teacher on part-time secondment.

The diversity is not confined to provision of staff and resources. It extends to the very nature of the centre's activities, and to the ways in which its basic aims are defined. Some centres concentrate on providing information about, and training in connection with, new curricular developments; they are more concerned, one might say, with disseminating new ideas than with giving them support once they have been taken up. Others seek to provide a service by building up a comprehensive archive of resource materials which teachers can come and inspect; supplying sample kits of materials to schools who want to try them out with a view to eventual adoption; and offering facilities for ordering films and videotapes, preparing slides and transparencies, duplicating locally produced back-up materials, and the like. Others again give particular encouragement to locally based development exercises, acting as parochial counterparts to national sponsoring agencies. A few aspire to more modest aims, and rely on attracting their clientele on a predominantly social basis, functioning more as a teachers' club (with periodic guest nights and celebrity spots) than anything else.

Teachers' centres which put their main efforts into local development are in fact closely reflecting one of the guiding notions behind their initial establishment: namely, to 'focus local interest and to give teachers a setting within which new objectives can be discussed and defined, and new ideas, on content and methods in a variety of subjects, can be aired.'[9] But centres of this kind can only be of very limited effectiveness in dissemination. The paradox which besets all local development exercises is that the more they succeed in enlisting the active commitment of local teachers, the more limited in their applicability the results tend to become. While major national projects may run the risk of alienation from real classroom concerns, they can foster worthwhile interchanges of ideas between teachers from a diversity of backgrounds. Localized development can very directly reflect local classroom problems but may pay the penalty of insularity and isolation.

So our main concern here must be with those centres which are more taken up with national than local curriculum programmes, and which seek to offer continuing support to schools engaged in the difficult task of translating new curricular ideas into practice. Such a centre can be most useful as an external source of legitimation and an independent reference point for innovative teachers who find themselves beleaguered in an apathetic or hostile environment. The Humanities Curriculum Project, in its dissemination phase, gave particular emphasis to 'local support meetings', many of which were organized by teachers' centre wardens. Some of the lessons learnt from this experience are likely to be of general relevance.

In her analytic review of the problems,[10] Jean Rudduck notes 'the tensions arising from a confrontation between schools', where one appeared to be coping more successfully with its difficulties than another. Here, she concludes:

It was important to contain competition by harnessing the differences in an exploratory, research-oriented approach. Teachers might . . . study together the effects of any moves that the support group had proposed in response to the problems encountered. . . . [She also notes] the associated difficulty of teachers describing experience in an honest and meaningful way so that the members of the support group could make a constructive response.

Because the more innovative-minded teachers were also usually the most heavily involved in other activities and the most mobile in career terms, many groups suffered from problems of commitment and continuity. But perhaps the most important finding of all was that:

If support groups have neither research interests nor practical tasks (such as gathering local materials, . . . developing a CSE syllabus, building a film library) then the meetings are likely to fold up after a while . . . groups, if they are to have a worthwhile life, must be capable of helping their members to function at the level of ideas – by formulating hypotheses and testing them in their classroom – and at a level of practical productivity.

By sharing his experience with those in other schools a teacher can be reassured that his difficulties in grappling with unfamiliar curricular problems are not unique; that 'instant success' is very rarely attainable; and that genuine and lasting change is hardly won. It can still, however, be important for teachers engaged in far-reaching curriculum development to be given some systematic form of support *within* the school. One of the most obvious ways of doing this is by encouraging close and regular collaboration between the group of teachers engaged in a particular innovation. Once again the Humanities Curriculum Project showed itself more sophisticated than its predecessors in recognizing and attending to this need. Jean Rudduck records that the Project strongly recommended that participating teachers should be viewed as a team rather than as a collection of individuals, and that one timetabled period a week should be set aside to enable them to meet for 'planning and reflection'. Though very few schools complied with this requirement, an encouragingly large number of teacher teams did decide to meet regularly in their spare time.

For obvious reasons, the attitude of the head teacher and senior staff is important. They can help secure money and facilities; they can encourage colleagues to accept and support experiments, and tolerate the initial difficulties. In contrast, if the 'establishment' is antagonistic even the most promising innovation may be slowly undermined. The sympathy of senior staff is worth enlisting, even by means of considerable effort.

So far, we have discussed local forms of support. There are other, less direct, means of providing continuing help. Where professional associations are able to identify themselves strongly with a particular reform, they can not only communicate the initial idea but also provide a powerful mechanism for its longer-term sustenance. For example, the Audio-Visual Language Association, the Association of Teachers of Mathematics and the National Association for the Teaching of English have each developed a very clear curricular ideology, and have backed up new curricular schemes which fit that ideology with a valuable network for the exchange of practical teaching experience. It requires an immense amount of time and effort for a development project to set up its own continuing support network from scratch; it is no mean bonus to be able to latch on to an existing one which has a proved ability to survive.

Because of the way many subject-based projects are organized and funded, the central project team itself will have disbanded long before the real need for a continuing support network arises. 'Aftercare' can, however, be provided where project development teams have become institutionalized, as the Nuffield science and mathematics groups have done at Chelsea College, London, the Nuffield/Schools Council language teams have done at York University, and some of the Humanities Curriculum Project staff have done at the University of East Anglia. The resulting curriculum development centres embody centralized expertise rather than practical working experience of the project's ideas and materials, and are therefore in a less good position than local groups to deal with detailed problems at the classroom level. They can, however, help to orchestrate the work of local groups and to sustain 'invisible colleges' of leading practitioners. They can also provide ancillary and revised materials where deficiencies in the original programme have come to light as a result of subsequent classroom experience. Central agencies of this kind do not compete with the teachers' centres and the schools themselves, but provide complementary forms of support.

A framework for curriculum dissemination

There are still two main areas in which significant improvements remain to be made before new projects can be spared the time-consuming process of re-inventing the support mechanisms of their predecessors.

The first issue to which more attention needs to be paid is that of the present reward structures for teachers. We have argued that the teacher's professional development is as important to heuristic curriculum change as the development of new curricular goals and materials. In most educational systems, however, salary and promotion arrangements are poorly designed, innovative work receives inadequate recognition internally and externally, and the necessary release time for further training and for local adaptation and development is not available. All these act as disincentives to thoughtful, well-informed and realistic response to change.

For example, it is often the case that teachers who have played a leading part in a curriculum scheme, either as part of the development team or as participants in the trial programme, are before long promoted out of the classroom into an administrative, advisory or training role. Their new post may well be in a different geographical area from the one in which their initial work was done. Their effectiveness in dissemination is then doubly neutralized – first by removing the credibility they would have retained as practising teachers, and secondly by depriving them of the network they have built up of personal and professional contacts.

Pay and promotion – though central to any discussion of incentives – are not of course the only considerations. It is important to take into account intrinsic as well as extrinsic rewards, such as the sense of satisfaction in a job well done, the appreciation of pupils and the professional regard of colleagues. In this context, as we noted earlier, the active support of the senior staff can be crucial. Yet here again, in the existing climate of many schools, curriculum change is seen as a threat to be isolated and contained, rather than as a legitimate and worthwhile concern capable of bringing added prestige to the institution as a whole as well as to the individual teachers involved. The effectiveness of curriculum development as a process must in the long term depend on the recognition of its validity by education officers, advisers, heads and others among those most capable of influencing teacher opinion.

The second issue which remains to be satisfactorily tackled in the context of the dissemination and adoption of curricular change is closely related to the first. Apart from inadequate career structures for those concerned with innovation and experiment, and the general uncertainty which surrounds the activities of teachers' centres as local agencies of dissemination and support, there is still a seriously inadequate provision of what might be called recurrent education for educators.

This seems an obvious need; indeed it has been formally acknowledged in a number of education systems in Europe and North America, though put into practice in only a few. A wise and balanced view of curriculum change can best be sustained by allowing teachers a regular rather than a sporadic and unpredictable series of opportunities to review new trends in their own fields of professional interest. This means in the first place creating special arrangements for in-service education, possibly along the lines advocated by the James Committee for England and Wales (including a 'sabbatical leave' entitlement for every teacher at five-year intervals), or along the lines already adopted by Danish schools (in which a full week outside termtime every year is spent by the teachers in further professional training). It must also – as we have already noted – mean ensuring that such provision is accessible to all teachers, and not simply to the particularly enthusiastic or the particularly junior. Finally, these two considerations of regularity and universality seem to imply a third: namely, that the provision for continuing professional development should be mainly school-based.

Certainly, if something along these lines were to emerge from the lessons of the past, the day would be nearer when the results of curriculum changes could be intelligently examined by the teaching profession as a whole, and when their dissemination need no longer depend on *ad hoc* arrangements. Nor would so much effort have to be put into constructing support networks for every separate scheme. The continuing maintenance of major projects need no longer depend entirely on individuals who move on or retire; the steady accumulation of experience and expertise could be built into institutions whose lifespan is likely to be a good deal longer than that of a single innovation.

9 Evaluating curriculum innovation

All manner of activities can be (and are) evaluated by formal and informal means. Within education itself, one familiar type of formal evaluation of individual students is through traditional examinations; and schools as a whole used, until quite recently, to be formally evaluated on a regular basis by HM Inspectors. However, distinctive procedures have been developed for evaluating curricular changes and this chapter will look at these.

As far back as 1949 Ralph W. Tyler spelled out a possible line of approach to the evaluation of educational programmes, as opposed to the calibration of educational performance (the latter being concerned with assessing students and the former with appraising their courses).[1] The origins of Tyler's early work lay firmly in the then current tradition of educational research, and more especially in psychometrics; indeed, it is only in recent years that evaluation has been clearly distinguished from research.

That the two have distinctive purposes should be obvious enough. The researcher tries to formulate and test general hypotheses about educational situations, and may well focus his search for common patterns on well-established practices. His subject is usually his own choice, and his results attempt to aid general understanding. In contrast the evaluator is normally commissioned by somebody else to undertake a particular study, in order that interested parties can make well-informed choices. His results are expected to provide useful information: to help show how some process is working and how it might be improved – which necessarily includes judging the merit or worth of the programme concerned. Such a study is usually of an innovative development, if only because these are subject to more rigorous scrutiny and questioning than accepted activities.

Any scheme of curriculum development involves a number of different groups of people who have an interest in its evaluation. For example, in the case of an heuristic project the development team will, in the course of the trial stage, need as early information as possible about which aspects of the whole are going well and which badly – and as much information as possible about the reasons why, in either case – so that they can modify their approach in the light of initial experience. The evaluator may be a member of the team, or work very closely with it, and his results may be irrelevant to the ultimate clientele because intended to be reflected in the final form of the proposals. This is usually termed 'formative' evaluation.

The teachers and administrators, in contrast, may prefer to wait and see examples of the changes in practice. Teachers will expect an evaluation to tell them what are the main pros and cons of adopting a project's recommendations, and what practical snags are likely to arise in a school with the particular characteristics which theirs possesses. Administrators will want first and foremost to have some indication of the costs, both financial and political, of authorizing adoption. 'Summative' evaluation, which is addressed to such consumers, looks back on a completed exercise and attempts to offer a balanced appraisal of its strengths and weaknesses. Here the evaluator will very often work independently of the developers, who may indeed have disbanded by the time the evaluation starts and will in any case be unable to act upon the findings.

In practice, the contrast is seldom as sharp as these theoretical distinctions suggest. Many studies commissioned to help a development team have generated ideas and identified sources of possible difficulty which are of at least as much interest to potential clients as they are to the developers themselves. Equally, some exercises designed to produce an overall judgement on a particular programme have given rise to subsequent remedial work on that programme, even though this has usually had to take place outside the scope of the original sponsoring arrangements. The important point is not so much that different types of evaluation take place at different stages in the life-cycle of a curriculum programme and have different intended audiences – it is that the business of the curriculum evaluator is to collect evidence about a given programme and to present it in a form which is both relevant and useful to those who have to make decisions about that programme.

The different styles of curriculum evaluation tend to match the different styles of curriculum development. An evaluator, being human, will not usually be attracted by the assignment of evaluating a programme with whose basic premises he is fundamentally out of sympathy. If his own outlook is somewhat technocratic, he will lean towards working on projects with similar value assumptions; if he is strongly humanistic in his emphases, he will show a natural preference for curriculum schemes with the same attitude; and so on. The parallelism can be traced in some detail through the recent history of subject-based development.

The problems of system-based evaluation

It may be useful first to look briefly at the notion of evaluation in the context of system-based programmes. Here the distinction in approach between evaluation and research becomes subtle, if not frankly blurred, though the difference of purpose remains. The goals of system-based curriculum reform are too widely drawn for the evaluator to attempt to measure a manageable number of specific outcomes, or assess a clear-cut set of desired skills or appraise a variety of identifiable processes, and to persuade himself (and others) that by doing so he will have provided a reasonably comprehensive examination of the scheme in question. Instead he has to rely on identifying what seem to be the most appropriate and sensitive 'indicators' of whether or not the scheme is working well, and then on arguing his case indirectly from these pieces of partial evidence. In the process he may often find it necessary to assemble statistical data, or to carry out large-scale measurement exercises, in a form virtually indistinguishable from his counterparts among the research community.

Where the evidence is inevitably incomplete, expert witnesses may disagree in their conclusions – as in the debate between Torsten Husén and Urban Dahllöf about the effects on pupil performance of the Stockholm comprehensive school reform. But a worse pitfall is that, because a system-based development usually has substantial repercussions on a whole range of educational activities, both its supporters and its opponents are more concerned to be proved right than to be given a fair picture of what is going on. The issues tend to become heavily politicized – and this means that, unless the evaluator is prepared simply to sell his services as an advocate for one side or the other, his activities may embarrass his sponsors and be seen as a positive threat by their antagonists.

In effect, the scale of system-based development is simply too large to allow for a balanced and comprehensive evaluation. Those promulgating reform naturally tend to insist that its effects should not be prematurely judged; so any evaluation which is officially sanctioned will be initiated, more often than not, some years after the new procedures have become established. They are then so entrenched that only exceptional individuals can have the political courage to question them. Usually, one of two things happens. Either the evaluation report is blatantly enthusiastic, applying liberal coats of whitewash to the finished product; or else it is mutedly critical, painting only a selected part of the whole scene in a dull shade of grey.

Perhaps in the contentious context of system-based reform, an impressionistic general critique of what is going on may be more useful than an exercise in formal evaluation. The polemic of the intelligent, committed and well-informed journalist may well be more apposite than the cautious agnosticism of the professional evaluator. To take only one example, Silberman's *Crisis in the Classroom*,[2] though essentially an argumentative caricature of the American school system addressed to the general public, has un-questionably had a greater impact than many of the more painstaking and detailed studies by those who earn their livings and make their reputations by curriculum evaluation.

In the light of all this it is scarcely surprising that most evaluators have preferred to assess the neat miniatures of subject-based projects. Within this tidier and more compact world there are three main areas on which emphasis may fall, in different degrees. The first is on the curriculum in theory; the second is on the curriculum in context; and the third, on the curriculum in action.

The curriculum in theory and in context

The evaluation of the curriculum in theory may be likened to the critique of an architect's blueprint for a building. It is certainly not irrelevant to ask of any curriculum design whether its proclaimed and covert ends are educationally justifiable; whether its proposed means are both feasible in themselves and consistent with the proclaimed ends; or whether the totality makes coherent sense. Evaluation of this kind can of course take place at a very early stage in the design process, when only the prospectus of a proposal is available: in such a case it is usually related to the decision of a potential sponsor whether or not to fund the programme as a whole. Characteristically, however, it occurs when the project in question has produced its initial materials. At this point the evaluative exercise becomes an amalgam between philosophical analysis and textual criticism: the materials are examined both for their epistemological form and their substantive content. The resulting appraisal may help the development team to revise their approach, serving as an *a priori* complement to the empirical evidence afforded by the field trials. But this type of curriculum analysis can also be applied to the finished products of a development programme, offering a balanced summary of the values embodied in the scheme; of its structure and its content; and of how far these accord. As such, it can serve as a useful form of consumer report to those individuals and institutions who are contemplating adoption but are concerned first to seek the guidance of an informed and reliable reviewer.

Evaluating the curriculum in context is markedly different from evaluating it in theory. Pursuing the architectural analogy, it resembles more the field activity of examining the finished building in its physical, social and economic environment. A very important element in a contextual evaluation of this kind – though the need has in the past been virtually ignored – is a study of the costs of putting a major curriculum proposal into effect. Costing studies of curricular programmes do of course call for the skills of a fairly competent economist; but it is less through lack of skill than lack of interest that the costing element has been neglected. Subject-based development projects first came upon the scene at a time when the economies of most Western nations seemed set for a period of growth. Alongside this, birth rates and education budgets alike steadily expanded year by year. Since the costs to any individual school or local authority of introducing a new curriculum scheme, however ambitious, were relatively marginal – a typical figure might be between 2 and 5 per cent of an adopting school's annual running costs – they could usually be met without embarrassment from growing capitation allowances.

In any case a number of the early subject-based developments were sponsored by private foundations – notably Ford in the USA and Nuffield in the UK – from funds entirely outside the normal education budgets. Economic evaluation became topical only when development costs were met from public funds. It seems likely that, in less opulent times, those responsible for managing the educational system will be more inclined than they once were to ask exactly what costs they will incur when a given school adopts a new project. This is not only because budgets are tight, but also because of the growing awareness that curricular change may demand, over and above the purchase of classroom materials, an extensive support system in the form of advisory services, teachers' centres and special in-service courses.

This is not the place to go into the technicalities of educational costing. It may, however, be worth making two comments. First, such evaluation exercises usually allocate the total initiation costs of development equally between the ultimate beneficiaries, distributing them over a reasonable period – say five years – while attempting to account for expected cost inflation and the interest the same funds might have accrued over this period. Commonly, the capital costs of installation (such as the purchase of equipment and materials, minor building works, and even in some cases teacher training provision) are also converted into annual expenses in the same way. The on-going costs of teachers, accommodation and the like will normally be shown in terms of costs per pupil hour for the subject in question – that is, the total estimated expenditure over the year will be divided by the number of pupils involved and the number of timetabled hours allocated to work on the curriculum scheme. This information, to make much sense, has to be supplemented by comparative figures, both for the costs per pupil hour of teaching the same subject under the previous arrangements, and for the contrasting costs of teaching other relevant timetable subjects, calculated on a similar basis.[3] Since such figures are not normally available in any school, a curriculum costing will often have the added bonus of disclosing to the head teacher and specialist staff concerned how much, relative to other subjects, a particular part of the curriculum enterprise costs to teach.

There is a temptation to go beyond this straightforward costing exercise to embark on a full-scale matching of costs with benefits. This amounts to an attempt to draw up a notional balance sheet, in which the costs which have been calculated are offset against the independently assessed advantages and disadvantages of the scheme under review, as translated into cash terms. What vitiates such an approach is the underlying belief that it is possible to put everything about a development project into the convenient terminology of pounds and pence. Even the most ambitious (and expensive) attempts by the US Office of Education to produce a plausible cost–benefit study of computer-aided instruction in the late 1960s and early 1970s, eventually produced no more than an apologetic explanation by the experts that the available techniques and instruments were inadequate (coupled, of course, with an assurance that if more research were commissioned, it would certainly do the trick).

The information which a costing exercise yields is of value not because it can be used in a simple balancing operation to determine whether adopting schools are getting their money's worth, but because it provides one more important piece of data in a complex exercise of judgement. To make any sense the quantitative has to be assimilated into the qualitative, rather than the qualitative being crudely reduced to the quantitative.

The other aspects of contextual evaluation – because more familiar than the economic component we have just discussed – can be more briefly considered. They constitute between them what Michael Eraut has termed a review of 'innovation strategy' (which he contrasts with 'curriculum strategy', or roughly what we referred to earlier as the curriculum in action).[4] Just as the pedagogy which results from an innovatory development must be open to the evaluator's critical scrutiny, so there is a case for looking at the effectiveness of such aspects of a programme as dissemination conferences and local and central arrangements for backing up teachers in the difficult early stages of adoption.

The evaluation of these features of a project's work is of direct interest to the central team and its sponsors, who will want to know which elements of the overall innovation strategy are most, and which least, effective. But it may also be of indirect interest to both the potential adopters and the teams and funding agencies concerned with future projects.

The potential adopters of subject-based schemes are themselves becoming more sophisticated in their demands. Many schools now realize the importance of some form of continuing support, just as many education authorities are aware of the needs for the in-service training of teachers and for readily available advice and guidance through teachers' centres. New programmes are expected to be accountable at least in part for such provision; so evaluation data on how effectively they meet it are as useful to the consumers as to the providers.

The steady evolution of different approaches to subject-based curriculum projects, as outlined in Chapter 5, suggests that successive development teams were quick to learn the lessons of the predecessors' mistakes. Much of this learning, as might be expected, took place 'through the grapevine': through informal anecdote and gossip rather than through formally authenticated documentary evidence. The techniques adopted in many early evaluation studies prevented their results from being produced quickly enough to be available to the projects which followed hard on the heels of the first cohort of subject-based developments. However, those more recent evaluation exercises which have included an element on innovation strategies have usually adopted a more directly informative and less measurement-based approach, and have been more concerned to make their results rapidly available. They have thus had some influence on the strategies of succeeding projects. For example, the well-documented approach to dissemination and implementation adopted by the Humanities Curriculum Project, and described in Chapter 8, has had a marked effect on subsequent practice. So the contribution of this type of evaluation to the work of sponsoring bodies and the curriculum development fraternity should not be overlooked.

Instrumental evaluation

We now come to the third and central component, the curriculum in action. On our architectural analogy, this corresponds with the building as it is lived or worked in; what actually goes on by way of realization of the architect's original vision. It will, for the purposes of clearer exposition, be convenient to look at the evaluation of the curriculum in action in its different chronological phases, and to link it with the earlier sequential discussion, in Chapter 5, of subject-based development.

Even in the early days of subject-based projects, curricular change was an obdurate topic for the established techniques of educational evaluation. The standard procedure was to compare the performances of two closely matched sample groups when one (the experimental group) was treated to the procedures being investigated and the other (the control group) received the normal provision. The two groups were tested after completing the necessary learning stages, and the sets of results were matched one against the other, often using fairly elaborate statistical techniques. As Parlett and Hamilton pointed out in a lively and polemical critique of traditional procedures,[5] this method appeared to derive from agricultural trials of new brands of wheat or clinical tests of new types of drug.

One basic flaw was its requirement that the end results of both the novel and the traditional process should be assessed in similar terms, the measure being the quantity of successful learning. Unfortunately, however, most curriculum projects were concerned from the outset to change educational ends as well as means. It was not just more efficient teaching of traditional content but an entirely new approach to the subject that was in question: mathematics as an understanding of basic concepts rather than as a set of numerical techniques; science as a process of inquiry rather than as a catalogue of memorized facts; languages as a living form of communication rather than as an inert decoding of literary works. So there could be no question of matching old against new on the basis of a set of performance criteria common to both; the amount of shared ground would in most instances be so small as to make a suitably fair test well-nigh impossible to devise.

So the would-be curriculum evaluators tried, instead of measuring the new in terms of the old, to judge each innovation against its own professed intentions. This approach fitted in neatly with the pure form of RD and D model, whose rhetoric demanded that the development process should begin with a clear and unequivocal statement of aims. The evaluator's task, as a good technician, was fourfold: first, he had to translate general aims into specific objectives whose attainment could be measured in behavioural terms; secondly, he had to devise a suitable battery of test items to assess how far students following the new programme actually matched its expectations; thirdly, he had to administer the tests in a suitably selected sample of adopting schools; and finally, he had to process the results of this testing programme in a form which yielded relevant and useful information, either to the team (in the case of a formative study) or to the sponsors or potential adopters (in the case of a summative exercise).

When the educational mood changed from one dominated by behavioural psychology to one in which the prevalent ideas were drawn from sociology and social anthropology, the popularity of this approach began to wane. But its decline was not only a matter of fashionable whim. Quantitative evaluation is powerless to reconcile the untidiness of actuality with the precision of the research ideal. To a quasi-scientific evaluator the schools appear as unmanageable as a Mad Hatter's tea party, occupying a world in which samples are never really representative, variables can never be held constant, and changes in behaviour – even if, as seldom happens, they can be accurately measured – do not adequately reflect the intellectual processes to which they are intended to equate. The raw data acquired in such studies are often suspect, because the measuring procedures are so crude; and it is no more appropriate to subject them to sophisticated techniques of statistical analysis than it would be to work out to five significant figures a calculation based on measuring an area of uneven ground with a yardstick.

An excessive or exclusive concern with measurement can also yield a distorted picture for other reasons. Important features may be neglected because they are not easily measurable. So the ultimate report may produce a detailed investigation of some particular effect which those involved in the situation, whether teachers or development team, may consider entirely trivial and beside the point. Moreover, a measurement-based study usually involves elaborate before-and-after testing schemes, and therefore has to be planned largely in advance; so it allows little scope for modification once it is fully under way. This, coupled with the fact that it is closely geared to the predetermined aims of the development team, means that it can take little or no account of those consequences of adoption that were not originally predicted, or of possible important side-effects on other aspects of the pupils' learning. If the initial hypotheses behind the project turn out to have been at all wide of the mark – which is not unlikely in anything as speculative as curriculum development – an evaluation programme designed on this *a priori* basis is likely to be limited in its usefulness.

A striking example was the evaluation of the Swedish IMU Mathematics programme, as much a model of its period as was the programme itself. The IMU scheme was an elaborate exercise in the development of self-study materials for pupils at three distinct levels of mathematical aptitude. The content was common, but the demands on the student differed substantially from one level to another. Changes in level between one module and the next could be made on the basis of carefully devised diagnostic tests. The idea was that, in adopting schools, the class teacher should step down from the lectern and assume the role of manager and tutorial adviser to individual students. Even more ambitiously, it was suggested that two teachers and a less qualified aide might between them cope with three standard classes of thirty pupils; it was argued that the resulting economy in salary costs would more than compensate for the extra costs of materials.

The evaluation study which accompanied the programme was generously funded and meticulously planned. It provided formative information which helped with the revision of the materials, and summative information which recorded, for the benefit of potential adopters, pupils' learning gains relative to those following traditional courses. But because it deliberately excluded any consideration of the subjective reactions of teachers and pupils, or the political context in which the trials were taking place, it totally failed to legislate for what did in fact happen.

Many of the pupils, after a lengthy period of exposure to working at mathematics on their own, became bored and restive; so although their measured progress in the subject was generally satisfactory, they gradually ceased to find any enjoyment in it. Few teachers, either, appeared to welcome their change in role from the oracular to the organizational. Meanwhile, the teachers' unions were currently in dispute with the central ministry over salary and employment conditions. The IMU scheme was seized upon as a convenient scapegoat, representing a clear attempt to downgrade the teacher in status, while at the same time heaping on to him more responsibility. With no one, except its originators, ready to spring to its defence the programme – which had been costly and ambitious in comparison with many schemes, highly successful on its own terms, and the subject of a detached and generally favourable evaluation – was quietly dropped.

But there was more to the story than that. The evaluation exercise also actually stultified the process of development. Before the trials had been long under way, the project team realized they ought substantially to rethink the initial design; they were prevented from doing so, because the costly and cumbersome monitoring machinery could not be disturbed. (The obvious alternative – which a number of team members took up – was to withdraw and set up a rival exercise, freed of the shackles of evaluation. This, though lacking official sponsorship, soon cornered the market.)

Experience increasingly revealed how deficient as a device was the measurement of learning outcomes. Two of the twelve case studies of evaluation reported in one of the early Schools Council research publications[6] record a realization during the course of the exercise that all was not going well, and a consequent shift towards a more qualitative emphasis. Writing about the Cambridge Schools Classics Project, Patricia Story notes that 'the marking of attainment tests in considerable detail occupied the evaluator for too much of her time, and some of the results obtained were not worth the effort expended on them; e.g. the analysis of pupils' mistakes did not affect the writing of the later stages or the revision of the material'. Wynne Harlen reported likewise in her study of the Science 5–13 Project. She subsequently went into fuller detail:

Information coming from children's test results was tentative and not readily useable for guiding rewriting without being supplemented by other data . . . for indicating changes which would make the Units more effective they were of much less use than information from other sources. The tests were also by far the most expensive item in the evaluation, both in direct cost and in man/woman hours . . . where resources are limited and it is necessary to concentrate upon gathering information to give the greatest return on money, time and human energy, then the choice would be for teachers' reports and direct observations in the classroom and not for tests of short-term changes in children's behaviour.[7]

The accompanying emphasis on clearly-specified behavioural objectives also began to seem dubious, for two main reasons. The first, as Wynne Harlen put it, was that 'these objectives will be constantly changing with the inevitable development of the project team's ideas . . . [the attempts to define them] could only be completely "successful" if the writers' ideas stood still – hardly a characteristic of a lively and creative team'. Secondly, teachers were hostile to any discussion of measurable performance criteria. Patricia Story records herself as meeting with 'a deserved lack of success' in her attempt 'to impose on a group of local teachers B. S. Bloom's analysis of cognitive objectives. . . . It was quite apparent from this experiment that any classification of cognitive skills would have to be straightforward and involve as little technical jargon as possible.' She was not alone in her discovery that most potential consumers find discussions of this kind of evaluation uninformative, if not unintelligible.

Interactive evaluation

The next group of development projects (with the Humanities Curriculum Project in the van) was less concerned with the progressive perfecting of packages of materials and more involved in improving the transactions of teaching and learning. So the evaluators' concern also shifted from accurate measurements of quantitative products to careful qualitative investigations of processes.

The new evaluators recognized that it was just as important to examine what the teachers and pupils themselves made of the whole affair as to study the developers' intentions. The resulting concentration on classroom observation and informal interviews with teachers and students has given rise to a series of closely related schools of curriculum evaluation, variously referred to as 'holistic' (MacDonald), 'illuminative' (Parlett and Hamilton), and 'responsive'

(Stake). The last-named has usefully summarized the main characteristics of this approach: 'it orients more directly to programme
activities than to programme intents . . . it responds to audience
requirements for information . . . the different value-perspectives
present are referred to in reporting the success of the programme.'

The first of these characteristics was taken to extremes by Michael
Scriven. Seriously or otherwise, he advocated a strange form of self-
imposed abstinence, in which the evaluator studiously avoided any
consideration of the intentions – either explicit or implicit – of the
development team, and concentrated entirely on the practical consequences of the work itself.[8] Such a procedure (which Scriven had
called 'goal-free' evaluation, and its detractors promptly nicknamed
'aimless' evaluation) was too artificial to win many adherents – but
the main point had nevertheless been made.

Concern with complexity – with 'the different value-perspectives
present' – is another salient feature of the illuminative approach. It
is well illustrated in the evaluation carried out by Barry MacDonald
and his colleagues on the Humanities Curriculum Project. The
development team were, in this case, relatively little concerned with
refining their materials, which were from the outset intended to be
locally modified and supplemented. They were more interested in
knowing what happened in schools which decided to experiment with
the project approach. Because they were anxious to underline the
experimental and exploratory aspects of their work, they refused to
define any objectives in advance; instead, they offered hypotheses for
investigation by the evaluator. So the evaluation study had itself to
be interactive, setting itself to explore the varied processes and
consequences of adopting the project materials, rather than simply
measuring the behavioural outcomes which might have been
intended as a result of using them.

MacDonald's study, along with others in the same interactive
genre, is sharply distinguishable from its more instrumental predecessors. Its population samples are chosen to be illustrative rather
than statistically representative. The atypical and abnormal result,
far from being averaged out into insignificance, is regarded as of
equal interest with, or even of greater interest than, the norm. The
investigator is concerned with trying to understand why things
happen, rather than simply with measuring what does happen; he
has to take into account teachers' opinions, classroom interactions,
and pupil's attitudes, motivations and sense of enjoyment – the
whole 'learning milieu' (in Parlett and Hamilton's phrase).

But even though the evaluator following this tradition goes into the situation with an open mind, he is expected to do a good deal more than register impressions in the way that a camera or a tape-recorder might do. His next task is to begin to identify key issues – recurrent concerns, unexpected anomalies, sharp differences in perceptions or values – and to focus on their implications in closer detail. Inevitably, certain ideas present themselves for further exploration: when these have been followed up, the question arises of how the results can be distilled and clarified, and to whom (if anyone) they are likely to be of major interest.

Out of initial complexity, so the hope runs, will come eventual simplicity – not so much a naïveté of content as a discovery of the most natural and appropriate means of communication. For this approach also pays close attention to its range of possible audiences and their needs.

Ernest House, in a characteristically trenchant paper on 'The Conscience of Educational Evaluation'[9] reminds us that:

We all live in a concrete world, in a world of metaphors and anecdotes, of strong feelings and personal relationships. Even evaluators live in that world. When I make decisions for myself it is on the basis of this concrete world, not an abstract one. The kind of information a person can act on must be meaningful in terms of personal experience. And that means appeals to metaphors, anecdotes, and self-interests.

Evaluators are not very good at translating abstract data, like correlation coefficients, into concrete experience for the audience. . . . In fact, the very methods that increase our generalising powers lead us away from concrete meanings into abstract relationships. There is a natural antipathy between personal meaning, which leads us into action, and abstract data. Communicating scientific findings is not a matter of understanding research terminology; it is a matter of translating the findings to fit the audience's personal experience. Every person has a vocabulary of action within his mind; only when evaluation data roughly correspond to his internal vocabulary does he respond to them. . . .

Ordinarily evaluators greatly neglect the 'context of persuasion'. However, it seems to me that the producers of the data must assume some burden in seeing their information is properly understood. Simply wrapping the baby up warmly and leaving him on the doorstep at midnight does not absolve one of responsibility.

The forms which evaluation reports take should therefore vary as their audience's needs vary. In practice, unfortunately, most evaluators of the interactive school have been little better than those adopting an instrumental approach in catering for anyone other than their fellow evaluators. But at least their style tends to be less inaccessible, and their subject-matter less devoid of human interest.

The approach has its risks. It is not enough that the evaluation should be acceptable to its audience. An impressionistic image of the personal perspectives of developers, teachers and pupils may be too diffused and anecdotal to be of real value: as Lawrence Stenhouse has pointed out, the aspiring novel may readily degenerate into a novelette.[10] Bias on the part of the evaluator, subjective assumptions and unexamined value stances, have somehow to be counteracted as well. This, though much easier said than done, is at least acknowledged as a problem, and is tackled by the technique of 'triangulation' – a grand-sounding term of art for the familiar process of cross-checking sources of data.

As this more open style of evaluation accumulates experience, it has begun to set its own standards and to develop its own kind of expertise. In December 1972 a number of its leading practitioners met in Cambridge at an invitational conference – sponsored by the Nuffield Foundation and convened by Barry MacDonald and Malcolm Parlett – to thrash out their main points of common agreement and mutual uncertainty. A whole series of activities followed, including the preparation of a volume of readings outlining the general approach and methodology favoured by the new school.[11] It culminated in the drawing up of a much quoted manifesto, which listed four main desiderata for future evaluations: that they should be 'responsive to the needs and perspectives of differing audiences; illuminative of the complex organizational, teaching and learning processes at issue; relevant to public and professional decisions forthcoming; and reported in language which is accessible to their audiences'. But the manifesto ended, with commendable frankness, by listing the main points on which no general agreement had been reached; and the last of these issues reveals a growing schism within the ranks of the faithful.

It holds open to question 'the degree to which the evaluator should interpret his observations rather than leave them for different audiences to interpret'. The issue of whether the evaluator should formulate and promulgate his own judgements or whether his proper business is to assemble and process the judgements of others may seem a fine point of theology – especially when it is set against the whole complex of distinctions we have already remarked upon between the instrumental style of evaluation and its interactive successor. But the distinction marks a basic doctrinal disagreement between those who recognize the job of the evaluator as being himself to evaluate, to be useful to his clients, to provide them with an efficient and serviceable set of recommendations for action; and those who aim, perhaps more ambitiously, to 'recognize value pluralism and . . . represent a range of interests', acting 'as broker in exchanges of information between groups who want knowledge of each other'.[12]

Obviously, an evaluator will find it hard to achieve complete transparency, to act as a pure medium which introduces no distorting effects. But it is a natural move on the way to a third, and relatively recent, approach to the problem of how an evaluation can come to terms with the uniqueness of the single instance.

Individualistic evaluation

We noted, in Chapter 5, that the interactive style of curriculum development had begun to be supplemented with a more individualistic approach, in which short, easily adaptable units of pupils' materials were prepared by the central team for use by teachers as they thought appropriate. Pupils could then work largely on their own or in small groups as they already do in many primary schools, with materials more or less closely geared to their individual capacities and concerns; the problems of teaching mixed ability classes in secondary schools might be eased.

Three main demands are made on the teacher by curriculum change centred on the needs of the individual learner. He must identify these needs, find facilities to meet them, and appraise how effective the results have been to the learner himself. The developer can help most directly in the second of these tasks, and the evaluator in the third.

But such a programme presents even more intractable problems for the evaluator than the interactive projects of the second main phase of curriculum development. Unless his efforts are to be spread very thin, he cannot possibly aim to offer guidance in respect of every individual student. While his work is necessarily carried out in a specific context, he cannot afford to let it remain limited to that context alone. He must concentrate, rather, in looking out for common patterns: for those types of learning need which often recur; for those situations in which particular resources or facilities usually prove helpful; and for those ways of enabling students to measure their own progress which generally seem informative to them. And he must use his findings not only to help developers to design resource materials which will be widely useful, but also to enable teachers themselves to take on a greater developmental and evaluative responsibility.

The basic tool of this third phase of curriculum evaluation is not the standardized performance test which dominated the first phase, nor yet the dossier of miscellaneous observational data geared to the 'needs and perspectives of different audiences' which characterized the second phase, but rather the carefully chosen, well-documented case study of the significant situation.

A case study can be more than a natural, indeed almost inevitable, means of gathering information about how a curriculum scheme is working. Set against a background of relevant experience, it can aspire to something of the explanatory, persuasive and exemplary power of the parable or fable. Argument by analogy is attractive; one of the strengths of the case study is its accessibility to potential audiences.

Gathering information is a good deal easier than picking out significant material from a welter of distracting detail. An unusually well-informed knowledge of current educational concerns is essential; so is discrimination and a sense of economy which can isolate relevant elements for thorough exploration. Above all, to tell the tale plainly and well, but with sufficient human interest to make it both relevant and engaging to a variety of publics, the aspiring case-study artist must have the narrative flair which can embellish the clear, classically sparse structure of the case itself with memorable detail.

This approach represents a move back towards research procedures – but no longer on the principles of agricultural trials. The individualistic style of curriculum development, and the case-study mode of evaluation which seems its natural counterpart, can be looked upon as attempts to formulate, test out and examine the effects of hypotheses about the learning process. Such hypotheses do not of course take the abstract form once favoured by behavioural psychologists – and the research, if it is to be so designated, comes at the applied, action end of the scale. Its distinguishing characteristics are the central role of the teacher and the unusually close partnership demanded between developers, teachers and evaluators.[13]

There is insufficient evidence as yet to judge the strengths and weaknesses of the case-study approach, but the technique may help resolve one of the dilemmas besetting curriculum evaluation. With the emergence of evaluators as a separate profession, with their own reference group, their own career structure and their own framework of technical concepts, language and literature, have come a better understanding of the problems of evaluation and more effective ways of solving them. But, in defending their professional identity, evaluators (including some of those who claim to act as honest traders in the judgements of others) have too often tended to ignore the fact that *all* those involved in the educational process are, in their own ways, evaluating that process. Many of the traditional agencies of curriculum control discussed in Chapters 2 and 3 have exercized, formally or informally, evaluative functions. Because they can take a view wider than that of a single institution, they may yield interesting judgements to set alongside those of teachers and pupils.

The development of case-study techniques may bring about a greater *rapprochement* between new-style evaluators and their traditional counterparts. The language of the case study is as familiar to Inspectors and educational administrators as it is to teachers themselves; indeed, it is quite naturally used by all three. Each can make a direct contribution to the process of case study evaluation, as well as direct use of its products.

Evaluating the evaluators

Of the three contrasting approaches we have outlined, then, the third is probably most effective in tapping the resources of evaluative energy latent within the educational system itself. What of the other essential resources of time and money? Sponsoring agencies naturally want an evaluation study to be done at a brisk pace within a reasonable budget. Developers need findings from trial schools to be reported within the limited timespan of a subject-based project. Finally, potential adopters will make their decisions on the basis of any evidence available at the dissemination stage; they will not wait three or four years for a formal evaluation report.

The orthodox objectives-based evaluation has proved slow and expensive. For example, the report of the very detailed study by the National Foundation for Educational Research on the Nuffield Junior French Project was not published until the scheme had been in general operation for almost a decade.[14] Its total costs ran well into six figures – rather more than the costs of developing the first three stages of the primary school materials themselves. In its quest for scientific accuracy and conclusive proof, this technique demands tests and questionnaires to be designed, applied to sizeable samples of pupils and teachers, and carefully validated. The conscientious evaluator cannot pronounce until mounds of data have been waded through and correlated. Some, indeed, have given up in despair, and potential consumers have perforce relied on anecdote and gossip.

The illuminative style of evaluation (usually associated, as we have noted, with interactive curriculum programmes) comes out somewhat better on the time-and-money test. The evaluator, because he is concerned more with evidence than with proof, is free to feed back his interim findings both to the development team and to the potential beneficiaries of the project. Because his study is progressive and cumulative, all is not lost if time and money run out. The main risk is that unless the evaluator is prepared to take some kind of interventionist stance, he may submerge his intended audiences in a sea of data – and this is only marginally better than giving them no data at all.

The evaluation of development schemes based on an individualistic approach is, in some respects, the most rapid and inexpensive of all. Detailed case studies of a relatively limited sample of individual learners can produce useful evidence at an early enough stage to be of value to both the potential consumers and the central team. A book of fables, or a collection of parables, can be built up gradually; no single item is useless on its own, though no collection of items can ever be counted complete. There, in part, lies the difficulty, because every bit of new data which comes to hand must modify and complicate the inferences which have already been drawn. It becomes progressively more difficult to generalize, as more case studies accumulate, about patterns of learning behaviour in relation to particular ranges of learning resources. Moreover, a case study by its nature has no real cut-off point. The unremitting pursuit of the particular can make heavy demands of time and energy, even if its costs are relatively modest.

Questions of value

One important point remains to be made. It is that, however much the evaluator may wish to abdicate from making value judgements of his own, he has to recognize that at almost every point education involves considerations of what is good and bad, right and wrong. If he is dealing with a project which attempts to modify or call into question the prevailing educational norms, he can neither take the project's aims as given nor write them off as unacceptable. He must explore, among other things, to what extent and in what ways some productive accommodation can be made between the two conflicting value systems. This inevitably draws him into the political arena, as particular causes look for support. Recognizing this, evaluators have become anxious to be 'sponsored but not bought'. They have come increasingly to favour a formal evaluation contract which spells out the scope and limits of their freedom in both initial inquiry and eventual publication, and which makes it plain to whom they are accountable and to whom they are expected to owe allegiance.

In his article for the Schools Council's symposium on 'current trends and implications' in curriculum evaluation, Barry MacDonald points out that the very style an evaluator chooses to adopt has its political implications.[15] He identifies three distinguishable stances which he labels autocratic, bureaucratic and democratic. It would be forcing the issue to equate MacDonald's distinctions very precisely with the three evaluation styles which we have identified in relation to the different successive phases of curriculum development. However, much of what he has to say about the autocratic stance accords quite closely with the respect for objectivity and the concern with scientific independence shown by instrumental, objectives-based studies; and the characteristics of his bureaucratic type are often found where an interactive evaluator accepts the responsibility for making his own judgements and for meeting the requirements of his audiences in a useful and serviceable way. But the closest fit is to be found between his notion of democratic evaluation and the non-judgemental modes of holistic, illuminative and case-study inquiry. Here, MacDonald stipulates, the evaluator's 'techniques of data-gathering and presentation must be accessible to non-specialist audiences. His main activity is the collection of definitions of, and reactions to, the programme. He offers confidentiality to informants and gives them control over his use of the information they provide. The report is non-recommendatory . . .'

Yet, despite the similarity in technique, there lies between MacDonald's 'democratic' and Stake's 'responsive' evaluator a fundamental gulf in policy. The one is totally subservient to his clientele; the other (as in an OECD evaluation conference in Liège in December 1974) may speculate whether or not the evaluator has a right – or even a positive obligation – to make sure that his recommendations are implemented.

Whether or not MacDonald's identification of the political issues helps to make sense of the complicated business of curriculum evaluation, it underlines the fact that it is not, and never can be, an exact science. Evaluation is a constantly evolving art, and necessarily influenced by the framework of values within which it is carried out.

10 The politics of acceptability

Change in the curriculum affects the lives, relationships and working patterns of teachers, and the educational experiences of pupils. It affects parents by altering the education which their children receive, and thereby confirming or challenging their own expectations of what school should be like. It affects the community at large, which is aware of the school through the outward conduct and attitude of the pupils, rightly or wrongly understood. It affects employers, who derive their view of the curriculum from a rough and ready measurement of how the abilities and aptitudes of the boys and girls they recruit match their requirements. It affects the post-secondary school institutions which take into their courses the products of the primary and secondary schools and are, therefore, sensitive to the consequences of curricular change.

Education is only one element among many in the complex mixture of social innovations which affect, say, parents bringing up children, or employers recruiting and training young workers; but it may be a handy and conspicuous scapegoat. And, of all aspects of education, curricular innovation most readily offers itself as the convenient explanation of specific evils. In considering, therefore, the politics of the implementation of curricular reform, we are moving into an area shot through with prejudice, fantasy and imprecision; we are trying, in what can all too easily be an artificial manner, to separate curriculum development from a range of other forces for change.

Teachers' roles

At the school level curriculum development challenges authority patterns and relationships between colleagues. The head teacher in the English education system has had a key role to play in the past, both as a force for innovation and as a barrier to change. In the primary schools the freedom of the teachers has to a large extent resided in the head. His or her philosophy has determined the atmosphere; he or she has guided the assistant teachers and super-vised their work, perhaps taking a direct hand in the choice of teaching materials and the selection of activities in the classes or teaching groups which compose the school. The head is the trainer and mentor of the younger staff, and his or her personal style of teaching has often provided a model for theirs.

The English stereotype of the autocratic head who has the power to initiate large-scale curriculum change, and whose leadership is backed by an acknowledged power to direct a professional staff, is in marked contrast to the role of the head or principal in, say, the United States or Sweden or Switzerland. It has aroused awe in visiting Americans, who have singled out the head's ability to push firmly in a chosen direction as one of the keys to the implementation phase of development. But what they have observed with envious admiration has been noted with polite distaste by Swedish visitors, who connect the large and potentially arbitrary powers of the head with the uneven quality of the education which is provided, and who question the independence of the head on democratic grounds. As for the Swiss, they find the role of the English head difficult to reconcile with a concept of professional responsibility vested in all teachers – a concept which enables elementary schools in Swiss cantons to function without any single member of the staff filling an authority role remotely like that of the head teacher in an English primary school.

But if the head is to implement major changes in educational method and internal organization, he or she must convince, en-courage or cajole the assistant staff to exercise their professional functions in hitherto unaccustomed ways. Many forms of curriculum development depend on changes in professional methods and assump-tions which are threatening to the teachers and which undermine the techniques and defences on which they have come to rely. It may be that young staff entering the teaching profession in recent years find congenial a more relaxed, less authoritarian style of teaching than would have been acceptable in an earlier period when the authority of age and status was more readily acknowledged. But team teaching and cooperative teaching – in the many forms in which these impre-cise terms are used – depend on the successful working out of staff relationships which cannot be fully predicted in advance. Part of the business of developing the curriculum at school level is to negotiate these changes. So personnel management is important.

To carry this approach too far is admittedly to end with a prescription for curriculum development by serendipity, or a total reliance on the emergence of the genius teacher or team of teachers. Even Sir Alec Clegg, who in his time was the most notable exponent of the 'genius teacher' approach to development, was also the most energetic and original in building up the in-service training network through which the experience of the 'originals' could be extended to the larger number of teachers who were ready to negotiate in their own way such complex changes in method, attitude and professional *persona* as might be required.

At the secondary level, the repercussions of curriculum change on the staff are magnified by size, and by the hierarchical and departmental structures through which the school is managed. Elizabeth Richardson has written at length on the application of a series of curricular changes in Nailsea, a large secondary school outside Bristol.[1] The school was a former grammar school in the process of going comprehensive; for three and a half years Miss Richardson doubled the roles of consultant and observer, as the head and his staff came to grips with the full implications of this change on the school's management structure, and the effects of a different set of pedagogic priorities on professional relationships. Her attention centred mainly on the conflict of roles imposed on the head and on other members of the staff, the pulls and pushes which develop when people are asked to step outside the boundaries they are accustomed to, or when they establish new territories in which to exercise their professional imperium.

This was a single case study, and it was presented from a particular psychological angle. Miss Richardson drew heavily on the experience of the Centre for Applied Research of the Tavistock Institute of Human Relations, using its own distinctive language and categorization, which some will find more helpful than others. But she was undoubtedly wrestling with the central issue raised by any attempt to organize curriculum change within a school. This is the question of how to create a style of leadership which satisfies the demands of management implicit in the size and complexity of the institution, while at the same time ensuring that all those affected by managerial decisions participate to the full. All this raises problems of human relations as well as educational policy, and the effectiveness of the school as a vehicle for a new curriculum depends on the skill and understanding with which they are handled.

With the curricular imperatives which must be accepted as part of becoming a comprehensive school, this may mean a change from a headmaster's autocracy, flanked by powerful deputies, to a form of cabinet government. It may alter the units of organization – upper and lower school, houses, year groups or whatever. It may mean changes in departments corresponding to changes in the way subjects of study are grouped together or separated. It may mean different forms of pupil representation, creating new legitimate ways in which pupils can test the nature and limits of authority.

Reference has already been made (in Chapter 7) to Countesthorpe Secondary School and Community College, which represents a deliberate attempt to plan a school in which the curriculum was thought out from scratch, or as near scratch as the exigencies of the system would permit. The affective and cognitive aims of the school required changes in the pupils' responsibilities for learning as well as in the way in which teachers related to pupils and to each other. Decisions on major and minor issues within the school rely heavily on the democratic institution of the moot (or council) in which teachers, pupils and non-teaching staff take part. New working arrangements had to be developed between the day school and the adult education element within the single institution.

Above all, the Warden (head) had to become a new kind of animal. He had to be able to lead, but with considerable subtlety and tact; to work through the loose, democratic, discursive, unauthoritarian, time-consuming apparatus by which the school made up its collective mind. He had to be the school's public representative, who took on his shoulders the community pressures which arose from anything controversial which the school did. And, with deliberately limited power, he had to sort out, negotiate and arbitrate the internal issues which nobody else could resolve. As a job specification it sounds impossible – and, indeed, the strain on the first Warden, Tim McMullen, Countesthorpe's only begetter, proved intolerable, as hindsight and Elizabeth Richardson might now lead one to expect. As the school has developed, so has the role of the head, and the strains have been moderated by the emergence of instant traditions and working procedures which have enabled new, less stressful, management techniques to evolve.

It is easiest to see the impact of curricular change on teaching styles, working relationships and authority patterns in such total examples as the transformation of Nailsea or the foundation of Countesthorpe, but it is not confined to them. The Humanities

Curriculum Project is also credited with far-reaching effects of this kind. The teacher's role here is to help pupils to learn from and assess controversial evidence of different kinds while himself remaining a neutral chairman. Experience shows that the teacher's attitudes are not modified only within the particular periods of school time set aside for the study of the HCP materials, but that when he is teaching other subjects, pupils regard him in a different light and he expects different things from them. His relations with other members of the staffroom, and his attitude towards staff participation in the formulation of school policy, are also altered. What begins as an attempt to discover a way of stimulating fifteen-year-olds of average abilities to learn by the discussion of controversial issues, eventually conditions teachers' responses to other questions.

The examples of both Nailsea and Countesthorpe suggest that one of the head's main functions is to gain and keep the confidence of the parents, making sure that their interests are not neglected in the professional arguments among the staff. The relationship between parents and teachers is one which has never been formally resolved. It is meant to depend on the trust of a client in a professional person. The implication is that the professional is more than an expert: he is an expert who is pledged to using his expertise responsibly on behalf of the client who places his affairs in his, the professional's, hands. Just as doctors command the confidence of their patients, and lawyers conduct business on behalf of their clients, so teachers (acting *in loco parentis* with regard to discipline and care) are trusted with the oversight and general direction of the child's education and the curriculum through which this is provided.

In fact, of course, much of what is claimed by professionals by virtue of their professional status is mumbo jumbo. The attempt to invest any professional activity – as opposed to other forms of skilled work – with the moral value implied by the notion of a special fiduciary connection seems to have more to do with the self-confidence of the profession and the faith of its clientele than with a rigorous analysis of professional conduct or roles.

Teachers are in a difficult position when it comes to making large professional claims. They are not independent operators. They work within a system answerable – in theory at least – to the public. They can claim responsibility for the curriculum only if it is also granted that a whole range of value questions are susceptible to purely 'professional' answers. No less serious, they practise an art which is difficult to evaluate; their pupils determine the teachers' success by their diligence, motivation, innate and acquired ability. There are no clear canons of professional behaviour: on the one hand, no legal action for professional misconduct is likely to succeed in the courts unless the misbehaviour of the defendant teacher has been so gross as to be culpable whether or not he was a teacher; on the other hand, the teacher can never offer the truly professional defence of his own actions which the surgeon puts forward when he says: 'the operation was successful, but the patient died.'

An educational covenant

All this has a direct bearing on the relationship between curriculum development – a high peak of the teachers' 'professional' activity – and the response of the parent as 'consumer'. Mention has been made in earlier chapters of the Schools Council's working party on the 'Whole Curriculum'.[2] One of its concerns was to devise an educational covenant which would protect the several interests of teachers, parents, pupils and society at large. As it stands, such a covenant appears to be a utopian gesture, but the issues which it treats are real enough.

Under the covenant pupils may expect to be 'treated with respect as persons', to have access to 'the widest possible range of all kinds of knowledge, arts, crafts and skill', to be equipped for employment and further learning. They can expect to be prepared for life in a democratic society, and to be given a non-sectarian introduction to the claims of religion. They can expect to be treated as 'responsible partners in their own education' and to be dealt with 'impartially and equitably'. Parents' rights are of a different order: they can expect to be informed and consulted on important decisions, to have their 'attitudes and values' treated with 'respect and understanding', and to be treated as 'partners in their children's education'. Society at large is credited with the right to 'expect the schools to equip their pupils to contribute to the community's economic well-being', to see children prepared for parenthood and for responsible citizenship.

These entitlements derive mainly from the responsibility which society places upon teachers to offer a worthwhile education to every child, no matter what their abilities, disposition or background might be . . . teachers in Britain have more independence than in almost any other country in the world. With this autonomy, however, goes a concept of professionalism which sees the teacher as not only having a high degree of competence in the classroom, but as having responsibility for his own educational aims and methods and, increasingly, for those of the school as a whole. In discharging this responsibility a teacher has to act effectively, and at the same time to acknowledge that there may be difficult conflicts of value between him and his pupils, their parents and society at large. . . . If he is to meet this responsibility adequately, and to develop the self-confidence which is essential to his effectiveness, he is entitled to count upon the support and understanding of the other parties to the covenant.

Support and understanding in this context meant the tools to carry out the job: better working conditions, more ancillary help and in-service training; respect for professional skill; and full participation in the development of the school's aims and policies.

British schools [the working party concluded] have for long been jealous of their independence in curricular matters. However much they may turn to outside bodies for resources, information and advice, they insist that the curriculum must be of their own making. We strongly affirm our support for this position. . . .

Such rhetoric from a working party composed exclusively of teachers and educational administrators sounded rather hollow at a time (mid-1975) when the notion of the teacher-controlled curriculum had already begun to come into question.

Simply to list hypothetical rights and duties does no more than point up the wide divergence, already demonstrated by the Schools Council's *Enquiry 1*[3] between the teachers' aims and the expectations of pupils and parents, notably about the vocational importance of schooling; and the similar gap noted by Musgrove and Taylor[4] which separates the pupils' idea of a good teacher from the teachers'. The covenant confuses a practical reality – the *de facto* control which the teacher exercises over the day-to-day running of the school (and therefore over important aspects of the curriculum) – with the public interest in the curriculum as a whole which must, quite properly, determine the limits within which teachers exercise this *de facto* control.

It is not that any of the propositions in the covenant is untenable, but simply that they belong to a particular kind of romantic make-believe. They seek, like another spurious social contract of the mid-1970s, to formalize moral obligations in quasi-contractual terms when, in fact, these obligations can only arise out of a set of dynamic relationships. They depend not on theory or law, but on energetic action, to make them a reality.

School and community

Parents impinge on schools in many ways and at many different orders of intensity. At a minimum level, they are involved simply by sending their children to school; at the opposite extreme is the parent who is co-opted on to governing or managing bodies, or who is active in the parents' association, or in some other way sets out deliberately to influence and be influenced by the school.

The character of the parental community and the social assumptions it embodies may, for good or ill, block the way to curricular change. One impression is that primary education in well-to-do suburbs is likely to be more conservative than in less favoured neighbourhoods, because parents are less disposed to encourage (or tolerate) teachers who want to change traditional practices. By contrast, it is alleged that in run-down urban areas where parents automatically send their children to the neighbourhood school, their inertia has enabled innovation to take place without the teacher innovators being challenged. Assertions of this kind are hard to substantiate, and are often designed more to support a polemic in favour of, or against, particular styles of primary education than to establish truth about parents and schools. The episode at William Tyndale School in North London in 1975 which involved parents, teachers, managers and local authority in a prolonged dispute, much of it about curriculum, crystallized when parents began to remove their children from the school and enrolments of new children dropped.[5] In this case, the social class characteristics of the school's catchment area were mixed: the individual protagonists were dramatizing issues which were of direct concern to parents of all classes.

What parents (not only middle-class ones) know of a curriculum may condition any choice they have of schools. They may warm to the approach to reading which a particular primary school is popularly believed to adopt, or they may sense an atmosphere of discipline or permissiveness which corresponds to their temperamental preferences. In the case of a secondary school, there may be parents who hold strong views on modern maths or new methods of teaching Latin, or believe the school offers particularly good courses leading to apprenticeship. All these choices communicate themselves to teachers and limit their freedom of action.

Most parents may in practice be more concerned with such wider aspects of the curriculum as discipline and expected standards of behaviour, than with subject content and teaching method. But as their children move through the school, parents encounter curricular choices which shape future opportunities, academic and vocational alike. A group of parents may come together and lobby the head to introduce French in a primary school or to adopt new methods and materials in a secondary school's science programme. More often their influence will be indirect or negative. Withdrawals and a declining enrolment lead to close scrutiny of the curriculum and to the suggestion that the head and staff are failing to satisfy parents. In less extreme circumstances rethinking may be stimulated after a parents' evening, when teachers become uncomfortably aware that parents are anxious about some particular aspect of the curriculum.

Holding on to parental support and interest has always been part of the head's job. Only in the most élitist and protected institutions have the staff been able to go through life oblivious of parents' feelings, and then only so long as the school has continued to thrive. For every cheerful buccaneer who has successfully ridden roughshod over parental sensibilities, there are half a dozen others who have run into difficulties. Traditional high-handedness with parents has been shown in practice to be less effective than persuasion and propaganda as a means of facilitating changes desired by the teaching staff. The course for parents on new mathematics seems to be a more promising headmasterly ploy than the lofty rebuff, delivered from behind a massive desk which – in rosy memory at least – once served as an adequate response to parental intrusion.

It would be a mistake, of course, to suggest that good management and tact can smooth over every controversy and satisfy every parent or group of parents. If the curriculum is seen to be a public issue, then parties will form on either side when opinion divides: the debate will become politicized, on Black Paper lines or on some other variation of the progressive–traditionalist division. Local newspapers are likely to join in as campaigning journalists recognize a means of dramatizing differences about major human concerns in the cockpit of a single school. Again, the early experience of Countesthorpe is relevant. As the new school tried to communicate its aims to the parents and the surrounding community, strong pro-Countesthorpe and anti-Countesthorpe lobbies formed in a matter of months, egged on by the local newspaper. The dispute continued, culminating in a formal inspection and the successful rallying of parental and community opinion behind the school, giving a further lease of life for the curricular principles on which it was based. The confrontation had to take place: there was no way in which the school could be all things to all men and remain true to its essential character.

There is nothing to suggest that, in practice, parents want to invade the schools or take over the prerogatives of teachers – or even to claim back with any stridency the powers and responsibilities the teachers arrogate to themselves in their more imperialistic moments. Normally the issue of where *control* should lie is not in question. This came out very clearly in the evidence collected by the Taylor Committee: what most of the advocates of appointing more parent governors wanted was consultation and influence rather than control. The composition of governing bodies may be symbolically extremely important; but on a practical day-to-day basis teachers and parents frequently come into conjunction on curricular matters in ways which need offer no threat to the teacher's view of his own professional autonomy.

The variety of approach to parents and community participation is indicated by the multifarious forms of the 'community school'. At one extreme there are community schools in which the main link with the community is in the use of the school building and sports facilities for community purposes (including adult education) – an arrangement which is intended to break down psychological barriers separating the 'teachers' school' from the community's building. At the opposite extreme there is the case where the staff set out deliberately to take the school to the community and bring the community into the school. In all this, there is the fairly simple idea that, as parents are partners with teachers in their children's education, one key to better learning may be found by involving the parents more directly in school activities. Often such changes will be made with the formal reservation that the curriculum remains the responsibility of the teachers. But if you give 'curriculum' its broad meaning 'involving the parents' inevitably means involving them in curriculum development.

It is the nature of things that the initiative in the community school usually comes from the professionals, not the parents. The local authority may have a policy for community schools (as, for example, in London, Oxfordshire, Leicestershire, or the former West Riding of Yorkshire) where adult or youth wings are attached to secondary schools. It will then be up to the head and his staff to show the local community and the parents in what way a community school differs from an 'ordinary school' – to open up the institution to the community, to involve it in local affairs, to offer its resources in connection with local social and cultural activities and so on. But a school which is prepared to ask the community how it can be open to community needs has to listen to the response it gets, and its own internal life is changed to the extent that it does so. This, indeed, is the object of the exercise. The school is not interested in community participation as such, but in mobilizing the support of parents so that school and home and the community at large can combine to forward the process of the children's education.

Of course, the community school can come to mean much more than this. It can be seen as an instrument of community development, in which educational goals are subordinated to the political aim of revivifying (and politicizing) a depressed inner city area and stimulating, through the cooperative opportunities for participation in school management, the unused energies and latent self-confidence of the urban poor. If and when this happens, the consequences are explosive. The professionals cannot then confine the enthusiasms (and conflicts) they have aroused to narrow questions of school management: curriculum content, allocation of time within the timetable and the appointment and qualification of staff will all become involved. Most of the examples of such parental activity would have necessarily to be drawn from North America,[6] but there is no reason to doubt that, given a certain combination of political, social and ethnic circumstances, similar episodes might take place in Britain.

In the English context the formal school remains the essential unit. Despite the wide scope for curricular initiative on the part of the schools themselves there has been little experiment with 'schools without walls' along lines made famous in the United States by the Parkway High School in Philadelphia. There an intimate link between education and the community has been organized by sending pupils out from a school base to receive tuition, not from teachers in classrooms, but from professional and other skilled people engaged in ordinary work. Thus those responsible for running the magistrates' court can supervise pupils' study of the legal process, the local hospital can provide the focus of a health education course, while banks, public utilities, local government agencies, industrial enterprises can all be used as teaching organizations for boys and girls pursuing individual or collective programmes under the tutorial supervision of their own teachers.

The absence in England of such community-based developments at the secondary school stage must reflect the teachers' energetic defence of their curricular autonomy which they are naturally reluctant to cede to individuals and agencies outside the school. In the United States or Canada the control of the curriculum is vested in public administrative bodies, and so teachers are more willing to share curricular innovation with non-teachers, and less disposed to exaggerate the 'professional' aspects of the task.

Consumers

Innovation in the curriculum also has to take account of community attitudes as they are expressed by the institutions which receive the products of the schools – industry, commerce and the public services on the one hand and higher and further education on the other.

How schools sort and sift generation after generation of young people – promoting some and holding others back so as to provide an operational élite for a technological society – is one of the main elements in the political debate about education, inasmuch as it reinforces or challenges the class and power structure of society. But the process (in particular the examination system which both controls the curriculum and grades the output) is also of interest to industry.

Many European countries recognize employers' requirements for trained manpower through the provision of vocational schools where skilled craftsmen are trained by instructors with industrial experience. As the move towards various forms of comprehensive education gathers pace, introduction to vocational skills is usually postponed until after the first cycle of secondary education is completed, at fourteen or beyond. But the needs of industry are an accepted influence on the content of the curriculum, following through the logic of a public curriculum which must prepare young people for the industrial and commercial life on which the economy and its social superstructure depends. And this, of course, is as true in collectivist Sweden as it is in individualistic West Germany. In Sweden representatives of industry and commerce and of the trade unions join with experts from the Labour Market Board in the negotiations and deliberations which are built into the preparation of the school curriculum.

As the public curriculum has not until lately been regarded as a suitable topic for public discussion in the United Kingdom, employers and trade unionists have had limited opportunities to bring their influence formally to bear. Such opportunities as they have had, they have taken. Both the Confederation of British Industry and the

Trades Union Congress have education committees which can collect and project a corporate view. They are represented on the Schools Council, albeit with a small minority voice. They are consulted when any major educational question is discussed by a departmental committee, or when, say, some major change in the public examination system is under consideration. The CBI takes a special interest in further and higher education, and the trade unionists consistently favour general education for all pupils as against the subordination of the curriculum to vocational interests. (The TUC position provides an interesting sidelight on the other debates about the common-core curriculum and differentiation in the secondary school referred to in Chapter 7.) But their influence on curriculum development has been small. The CBI's constructive scheme for introducing teachers to industry during school vacations does certainly affect teaching and extend the range of what is taught, informally as well as formally, but the scale is minor. Nevertheless, their continuing involvement is signalled by the fact that both the CBI and the TUC have joined in a social studies project organized by the Schools Council on the world of work.

At more informal levels, employers help to form the external climate within which the schools operate. Ritual attacks on schools and universities for their failure to provide students with adequate basic knowledge or a favourable orientation towards industry may appear to have little direct effect upon those institutions. In most cases they are not statements about education at all, but about politics and the state of the social revolution. But when they connect with larger anxieties within society as a whole, the combination may produce reactions which narrow marginally the schools' range of curricular options. Moreover, an informal influence is the schools' own belief in the existence of an employers' view and the need to serve industry. For instance commercial employers (as well as university engineering departments) are alleged to dislike the new mathematics because they think it fails to teach basic arithmetic: and this supposition may lead to syllabuses being modified.

The employment situation is also likely to be a very present influence on pupils and teachers at local if not at national level. Here again, as in the case of the community school, how the pressures express themselves will depend on the character of the area, the range of local employment, and the educational attainments of school leavers. More and better careers-teaching – another curricular innovation – has opened up some schools to the world of work; at the same time, the head's erstwhile patronage in supplying local commerce with bright fifteen-year-old lads to fill vacancies in the office has diminished as more pupils stay on at school after the minimum leaving age. Work experience, and courses linked with further education colleges, are other developments which have extended the indirect influence on schools of the industrial and commercial community. The raising of the school-leaving age to sixteen stepped up attempts to develop closer contacts between school and employment, and the recession of the 1970s made schools more conscious on their pupils' behalf of the looming prospect of job-hunting. The dominant aim of most academic education, however, has remained to postpone vocational commitment and equip pupils with the necessary resources to pick and choose from a range of occupations less vulnerable to booms and slumps.

At the further education level the most significant development of the recent past was the establishment in 1973 of the Manpower Services Commission and its offshoot the Training Services Agency, sponsored by the Department of Employment. The main impact of an energetic, centrally directed and financed policy for skill training will be in the colleges of further education. But there will also be backwash in the schools. True, the Department of Education and Science has made efforts to defend the status quo of local education administration and local curricular autonomy. When the MSC/TSA discussion document on *Vocational Preparation for Young People* (1975) criticized the educational preparation of school leavers and remarked on a need to provide remedial courses for young workers in basis literacy and numeracy, this was perceived as another threat to invade the 'secret garden of the curriculum'. But this was only to be expected, if the schools are recognized to be temporary custodians of the curriculum, not owner-occupiers.

Professional bodies – which limit and control entry to more or less exclusive guilds on the grounds of educational qualifications – exercise a direct influence on post-secondary institutions which may wash back into the schools. For example, the Council of Engineering Institutions has taken steps over a period of years to restrict entry into a wide range of engineering activities to those who have pursued a lengthy course of full-time study in an institution of higher education. Here a well-remunerated professional group is clearly trying to improve its status by restricting access to its mystery. It fits into a larger pattern of interlocking actions and reactions to an expanded system of higher education. It has the effect of influencing the curriculum in many institutions by excluding part-time students and increasing the emphasis on the academic over the practical. It thus helps to shape secondary school expectations as well.

It is commonly believed that the universities, and the rest of the apparatus of higher and professional education, exercise a powerful influence on the secondary school curriculum and impose constraints on its development. And in so far as people in the upper secondary schools hold this belief, the universities probably do exercise such an influence. Even though less than 10 per cent of school leavers go on to university, the university expectation and the structure of public examinations built upon it has helped to shape the pattern of sixth-form studies for many more. So, too, have O Level requirements, which are meant to establish an intermediate level of general education on which pre-university studies are built. The long-drawn-out discussions of A Level reform, in Schools Council committees and in the Standing Council on University Entrance, provide a measure of the seriousness with which this influence has to be taken.

As was indicated in Chapter 3, the direct influence which academics exert on examinations through their membership of the Schools Council and in the O and A Level examination boards is probably less than the indirect, through the number of university staff who supplement their incomes by serving as chief examiners and as examiners at A Level. But at critical moments they retain a direct influence: the view of a university examining board on a proposal for examination reform carries with it some of the university's own prestige.

There has, however, been little evidence of official university pressure on subject-based curriculum development. Professor McGlashan of the University of Exeter Chemistry Department, for example, who announced that he would not accept the Nuffield Physical Science option in A Level as a satisfaction of the faculty requirements for entry, stands out as a distinguished eccentric. On the other hand, faculties which are oversubscribed can no doubt discriminate between those A Level courses they like and those they distrust; and there is a certain ruthlessness about each university's single-minded quest for the best students, which the schools themselves understand well enough.

This affinity between the teachers of university candidates in the sixth forms and the university teachers who admit them, is the most powerful instrument by which higher education dominates the academic programme of the upper secondary school. The main control is in the minds of the teachers. They take with them, from their own higher education, assumptions about the nature and content of their chosen field of study which they incorporate in their approach to specialist teaching in the secondary schools. When they guard standards on behalf of the university they are guarding their own standards; when they defend this or that ingredient in a specialist course in the interest of the continuity of undergraduate study, they are reflecting their own professional formation. They may not actually be more royalist than the king, but the evidence suggests they are not much less so.

Graduate teachers' preservation of their intellectual inheritance transmitted via the universities has a direct parallel in a country like France, where a well-understood, high cultural tradition exerts a powerful influence – in many ways more powerful than the centralized state authority which is nominally in full control.

If the schools are influenced by the examination requirements set up by the universities and polytechnics, the universities themselves are more likely to change their courses – or invent new ones – if student demand falls off than because industrial and governmental employers complain about the education and attributes of graduates seeking employment. Without a healthy level of recruitment, the university is in trouble and its grants are threatened. By comparison, kind words from large employers butter no parsnips.

When students cease to come – when, for example, classics ceases to be able to recruit students with a working knowledge of Latin or Greek – then it suddenly becomes possible to accept lower levels of attainment than those hitherto regarded as essential to higher education. Classics dons accept the change and show remarkable flexibility of mind because their livelihood and status is at stake.

This is paralleled in the secondary school. When students can no longer be persuaded to choose Latin, large numbers of otherwise redundant Latin teachers become converted to courses on classical civilization; and obstacles in the path of this particular curriculum development melt away. As the same progression of events overtakes modern-language teaching in the comprehensive school, a similar curricular mutation takes place, from German and Spanish to contemporary European studies.

Of course, students may desert particular disciplines as a delayed response to employers' lack of enthusiasm. Lower recruitment rates to Swedish universities at the end of the 1960s were widely attributed to a rise in graduate unemployment and a decline in the income differential enjoyed by graduates – which is highly relevant to the repayment costs of student loans. But the process by which the message is picked up by students is largely a mystery.

Teachers, parents, pupils, politicians, employers and post-secondary consumers of the product of the education system – each has an interest to defend, a susceptibility to be respected or ignored. How the various groups interact in respect of curriculum development reflects its public character and the dynamic relationship between education and society. In the final chapter we shall attempt to look at the dynamics of the curriculum debate in the light of what we have written so far.

11 The dynamics of the public curriculum

It is a basic premise of this account of curriculum development that the curriculum itself is not static but dynamic. It is a response to many different pressures outside the educational system. These pressures change. Economic and technological development create new demands, modify old ones, and change the social environment in a variety of indirect ways. Social class boundaries shift. The family adapts to changes in working life. More wealth means better health, more leisure, more mobility, more independence, less cohesion. Against this changing background, religious and political passions ebb and flow. New psychological insights, appropriate to the social expectations of the time, bring changes in attitudes towards the young. Formal political activity translates into educational terms a continuing quest for social justice. In short, what happens in school is an indirect expression of what is happening in society.

In previous chapters we have been concerned with how these external pressures have been transmitted to the schools, with attempts to adapt the curriculum more effectively to present and future needs, and with the many different agencies which influence and control the curriculum. We have tried to indicate that curriculum development is therefore to be approached at many different levels. A piece of orchestral music can be approached in terms of the score for each individual instrument. When the whole is considered, when the orchestra is assembled under its conductor and the music emerges from the perfectly matched *ensemble*, this is something else again. The application of the analogy to curriculum development breaks down at this point, because there is no conductor. Even in highly centralized education systems, central direction cannot bring about a perfect *ensemble*. In more or less decentralized systems there is no direct way in which a central authority can command the attention of every participant; in England it has hardly been attempted. Instead, an array of separate, conductor-less groups improvises to a score imprecisely drawn within certain guidelines determined in advance by committees of instrumentalists and administrators.

There is no serious suggestion in the United States that the Secretary for Health, Education and Welfare should assume control of the curriculum. Nor, though there has been a perceptible change of mood, are there many who believe that the Secretary of State for Education and Science in England and Wales could, or should, mount the rostrum, tap his baton on the music stand and call the players to order. For historical reasons the distribution of power and initiative on the curriculum has become a tradition which English teachers and educational administrators now regard as a cornerstone of the educational edifice. Perhaps this is more than habit: some of the best and most creative features of the English education scene are claimed to be associated with this wide distribution.

As we have seen, one response to the decentralization of curricular responsibility is to concentrate attention on the component parts of the curriculum, rather than on the whole – as it were, on the scores used by individual instrumentalists. Subject-based curriculum development has been relatively easy for both the developer and the system to handle. It has been possible to involve large numbers of individual professionals in the development process, to implicate them in decisions and choices, and to negotiate with them new guidelines which can eventually be given the form of alternative examination syllabuses for the subjects in question. And, because the outcome of subject-based change has always been a new course or a new approach which every individual teacher could take or leave as he chose, the great majority of teachers have simply stood by and watched what was going on as sceptical but not acutely hostile spectators.

In many ways, the absence of hostility is a measure of the ineffectiveness of the process. Yet had it been more effective, the balance of power (which depends on a consensus) would have been upset; and nobody has had the mandate, nor yet the desire, to bring about such an upheaval, let alone to clear up the debris afterwards. It would certainly be hard to show conclusively that some specific alternative recipe would be more efficient than the present muddled consensus, given that any alternative would have to be operated after the curricular revolution by the same people in the same circumstances as before.

The Schools Council is an example of one attempt in a decentralized system to organize development on a non-directive basis. It is one of an international genre of national development agencies, and faces the inherent problems of all such agencies. How, above all, is it to draw into curricular issues a wide range of interests, from outside the schools and hitherto unrecognized by the English educational establishment?

The Schools Council assumed in its first phase that the curriculum was the private fief of the teachers. The teachers' trade unions had the leading voice in its first two constitutions. By promoting this myth the Council thrived for a time, but in doing so demonstrated that for vested professional interests to attempt to keep politicians away from the curriculum was fundamentally undemocratic. The third constitution (1978) clipped the unions' wings, thus also signifying the more modest role the Council would play in the future.

School-based development

Because of the obvious limitations of the subject-based forms of curriculum development and because (for reasons which were explored in Chapter 6) the English educational system does not lend itself to coherent forms of system-based development, much recent curriculum development has concentrated on the school level. A new head, or an old head invigorated by new enthusiasm, gathers round him a staff prepared to think collectively about the needs of the pupils in their care, and devise and apply to the school a curriculum they deem appropriate.

Many of the obvious examples concern attempts to devise new curricula in new schools. For instance, a former Schools Council Joint Secretary, Geoffrey Cooksey, took the *tabula rasa* of the timetable for the schools on the Stantonbury campus at the new town of Milton Keynes in Buckinghamshire, and assembled a programme of study and activity which draws together in a new package both the fruit of development undertaken elsewhere and custom-built self-instructional study materials. His job was to plan a curriculum for local children which reflected both their needs and the strengths and skills of his staff. The school had to fit into the larger framework of the public curriculum for English secondary schools – that is, a sizeable proportion of the pupils had to be enabled to succeed in public examinations and find their way at the appropriate level into post-secondary institutions, and those who finished their education at sixteen ought to get reasonable jobs.

Such eclectic and locally relevant curriculum development is much more likely to penetrate the individual classroom and be accepted by the individual teacher than anything engineered by remote control. It capitalizes on both the skill of professional curriculum developers and the personal convictions of the teachers directly concerned. Within the special circumstances of a new school a consistent, integrated programme of study and all kinds of school activities can be planned to fit predetermined educational goals.

But school-based curriculum development also very clearly shows how far the head of a school and his staff – temporary incumbents of a public institution – are able and encouraged to stamp their own values on a school. The public curriculum is a flimsy and insubstantial framework, even at the secondary school level where there is still a public examination system – and the more examinations are controlled by teachers the flimsier it will become.

It also tends to obscure the national importance of the value judgements implicit in curriculum development. Like other forms of piecemeal development, school-based reform enables the system to change little by little, a boundary extended a few yards here, a quick strategic withdrawal to an earlier baseline there. It enables apparently scandalous innovations to become familiar; it fits into the established English pattern whereby almost any outrage becomes a tradition if it can be nursed through infancy.

But heightened interest in curriculum development has led to new challenges to the traditional consensus: those who reject the social status quo criticize the sifting process by which schools maintain it. The politicization of the curriculum debate is a direct reflection of the politicization of other aspects of social policy. There is no way of insulating education against this, even were it desirable to do so. Indeed the present agencies of curriculum control and development were brought into existence to make sure that what happens in school is responsive to just this kind of transformation within the social environment, and to discover new conventions strong and flexible enough to contain and harness the potentially explosive forces thus released.

School-based development may also avoid the issue of where responsibility for the curriculum is to lie. Take, for instance, the value attributed in one school to competition and the assumed antithetical value which another places on cooperation. The typical progressive head will play down such remnants of the *ancien régime* as form orders, marks and school prizes; his classes will be un-streamed and work organized on a group basis as far as possible, where the strong can help the weak. A more traditionally minded head will attempt to carry into the comprehensive school the expectations of the grammar school: he will maintain that streaming is necessary to efficient class teaching, and that competition brings the best out of pupils as they strive for approval and good marks. Neither head necessarily reflects the views of his pupils' parents – though, because many parents have a mental stereotype of school which more nearly resembles the vision of the traditionalist, they are more likely to revolt against the progressive. But there is still a doubt in principle about whose will should be imposed on whom.

Nor is it only in respect of political or social philosophy that difficulties may arise. There is the more general objection that school-based curriculum development reflects the limitations of sympathy, understanding and cultural bent (not to mention technical skill in course construction and preparation of classroom materials) of the handful of individual teachers who happen to form the directing group at the top of the school. What if these sympathies and under-standings are too narrow, or if the collective cultural orientation is unbalanced or eccentric? In terms of curriculum development, important issues hinge on the range of choices which individual pupils are offered at critical stages in the secondary school course. The teaching profession is orientated towards academic study rather than the world of work; towards pure science rather than applied science; towards the arts and social sciences rather than technology and crafts; towards the reproduction of its own species rather than the creation of a new generation of wealth-producing engineers and entrepreneurs.

There is enough truth in this argument to suggest that even when teachers think they are planning the curriculum on objective 'educational' grounds, they are shaping it in a way which begs a wide range of questions, some of which may be of great significance to the national life as a whole. Leaving individual teachers to settle what should be done relieves everybody else of the responsibility, but does not necessarily help the education system most effectively to contribute to the solution of national problems.

There is, of course, the saving grace that schools are splendidly ineffectual institutions and that exposure to any particular political or educational ideology at school can lead to diametrically opposite attitudes and values in later life. But they become even less effectual

if the school's curriculum and the teachers' ideology is so controversial that eventually parents and the local community cannot
stomach it. If children are taken away and sent to other schools there
is inconvenience for parents and children alike. Dissension in the
staffroom undermines the efficiency of the school, even within the
terms of its own ideology. In the ensuing muddle and mud-slinging,
reputations are destroyed and public and private persons behave in
ways which do them less than credit. The results of such curricular
shambles can be seen in the unhappy stories of Risinghill in North
London in the 1960s and Summerhill in Aberdeen in the 1970s –
schools in which the local education authorities with great daring
appointed controversial heads whose educational philosophies were
likely to arouse at least initial, and perhaps, lasting, hostility; and
later refused to support them – perhaps rightly – when difficulties
arose among staff.[1]

Towards clearer national guidelines

All this seems to have implications for the future of curriculum
development generally, and especially in decentralized systems. The
international upsurge of interest in educational innovation in the
1960s produced the inevitable reaction of scepticism and distrust
from the community at large, which had never shared the curriculum
developers' touching faith in the benefits of change. One manifesta-
tion of the backlash was increased public anxiety about 'the basic
standards' of education (a down-to-earth expression of concern
about the curriculum which comes easily to politicians, both local and
national). In the United States this has often led to the introduction
of regular testing at different age levels throughout the period of
compulsory schooling. A brief flirtation with performance accounting
– the modern equivalent of payment by results – was successfully
fended off by the teachers' unions and discredited, but state legis-
latures such as those in Michigan and California went ahead with
laws which had the effect of setting standards for teachers as well as
pupils and deliberately imposing external pressure on the school
curriculum.

Nothing so dramatic occurred in Britain; but there was a similar
questioning of basic standards, and a similar request for account-
ability. Disillusion about educational innovation was personified in
the arrival of Mrs Margaret Thatcher as Secretary of State for
Education in 1970, who brought with her a strong and instinctive

distrust of the Schools Council. The setting up of an Assessment of Performance Unit was, it is true, studiously calculated to avoid adverse professional reaction: virtually nobody in Britain wishes to replace a decentralized education system with rigid centralization. Nevertheless, it has become obvious that the present interpretation of the roles assigned to the various agencies concerned with the curriculum is unsatisfactory. For a start, a careful look is needed at each of these roles. Those which have become blurred and fuzzy at the edges will need to be sharpened – otherwise the weakness of the national curricular framework must, sooner or later, threaten the practice of local curriculum development. Local school-based development is only tolerable within limits; but the setting of limits has gone out of fashion, and it will require tact, skill and determination to re-establish them.

This is no more than a reflection in educational terms of the eternal paradox of law and freedom. One of the effects of curriculum development itself has been to question the assumptions and traditions of the educated minority which has for years formed the framework of the educational system. Other aspects of society are likewise being forced to replace unspoken conventions with more explicit expressions of national purpose and policy. When an administrative élite which shared the same universities, schools and clubs, could count on others outside the charmed circle to take a lead from them, a great deal could be left unsaid. As this tacit consensus breaks down, it can be no cause for surprise that more legislation should be needed, or that areas of human activity hitherto governed by convention and an implicit sense of form should need a more explicit set of rules – even if this same breakdown of one set of social regulators makes the task of getting another more contentious.

It was inevitable that growing government interest in the public curriculum should highlight examination reform as an obvious place to begin the re-shaping of the Secretary of State's role. With the reform and management of secondary school examinations must go a greater readiness to ensure that the secondary school curriculum across the whole of the system has some coherence. A symbol of this might be for the Secretary of State to be empowered to prescribe in general terms the core subjects which should occupy, say, at least half of the school timetable up to the leaving age. Of course, an ingenious teacher could justify a very wide range of activities under the general heading of English or science. But the gesture would signify a shift in the conventional wisdom.

The way would then be paved for a review of the role of Her Majesty's Inspectors, and for their emergence from the recessive shadows of the recent past. They need not don the authoritarian mantle of the Victorian school inspector, but certainly they might put their eyes and ears more effectively at the disposal of the Secretary of State. Everything suggests that there will still be times when the full powers of Inspection may be needed, and when teachers and l.e.a.s alike will welcome the judgement and advice of well-qualified and experienced professionals from outside. It might be expected, too, that the Inspectorate would return to the preparation of guidelines on various aspects of the curriculum. These need not offer detailed instructions, nor need they be presented as the binding standing orders for each school's curriculum. But they would have the status of an official record of public expectation, helping to form the basis of local reviews of curriculum, in which the HMIs could themselves take part. Here the Inspectorate would come closer to the Schools Council's field; but there seems very little reason why the *Handbook of Suggestions for Teachers* should not be reissued in some new form.

Developments along these lines at the national level would also assist the local education authorities in improving their own advisory teams. If school governors and managers are to be strengthened, and encouraged to play a bigger part in the policy-making of individual schools, l.e.a.s will need to develop the support services to help put right the deficiencies to which they will certainly draw attention. In the inevitable confrontations between professional leadership and lay management both parties – the head and his staff and the managers – must be protected by the right to draw on the trouble-shooting capacity of the local inspectors and advisers.

Local education authorities need also to accept the responsibility of tackling curricular questions when these surface in public dispute, and therefore to be more ready to involve themselves at an earlier stage to prevent confrontation. The official post-mortem on the William Tyndale junior school dispute in North London showed in exhaustive detail how the divergent views of teachers, parents and managers produced a specific conflict which the Inner London Education Authority was not willing to resolve.[2]

London had an inspectorate as well staffed and qualified to carry out the investigation which was required, when it was required, as any English l.e.a., but there was a reluctance to acknowledge that it was the job of an education authority to sort out curricular disputes.

An important part of the report on the public inquiry was devoted to an interpretation of the legal responsibilities of the authority in curricular matters, both generally and with reference to the rules of management under which they set up managing bodies. Its author, Mr Robin Auld, concluded that they were legally obliged to reassume all the powers they normally devolved to the school level if the managing body failed to exercise them, or was unable to exercise them satisfactorily. With a shrewd legal finger he pointed out the lack of legal substance in the myth of the teacher-controlled curriculum; and his conclusions apply beyond his London context.

The William Tyndale episode offers a case study of innovative failure. It exemplifies, among other things, inept teacher-controlled curriculum development; an impotent local authority inspectorate; failure by the local authority to accept responsibility for the curriculum, leading to the eventual collapse of the school when parents, teachers and managers pulled in different directions; the failure of the staff to carry the support of the parents, and the reluctance of the staff to compromise their own professional principles by seeking to persuade parents; and the consequences of internal staff division.

Curriculum development in the round

It has been part of our thesis that the nature of curriculum development can only be properly understood if the curriculum is interpreted very broadly, as an interlocking set of activities which extend far beyond the narrow limits of subject syllabuses and timetables. What has manifestly been lacking is a realistic appreciation of this in Britain at the level of the central government. Any tuning up of the present mechanisms for controlling the curriculum which failed to adopt a wider view would almost certainly achieve results so trivial as not to justify the effort. An effective tightening of the strings would doubtless be represented as hostile to the idea of curriculum development as such; but in fact it may be a necessary condition of its continuance. It must entail serious debate at the centre about which main lines of development ought to be encouraged; as we have argued, it is insufficient to concentrate on one facet only. So far the Schools Council's curriculum projects and school-based developments have dealt with 'downstream' issues – the working out of new courses, and the integration of new courses and combinations of courses into a single school. There has been little if any coherent thinking about the 'upstream' questions which can only be settled out of the reach of the individual school or team of subject specialists.

Reference has been made to the argument about the balance between arts and sciences, and between pure and applied sciences. The official doctrine, articulated in the Robbins Report of 1963, is that the educational system should be responsive to the private choice of millions of individual pupils. Policy for university expansion in the 1960s made certain assumptions about the balance between places for science and technology and for arts and social sciences; but the opponents of manpower planning held sway, and any attempt to influence applicants' choices was held to be misconceived because nobody knew enough about the future to say, in advance, which choices were going to be best or most appropriate.

But still those millions of individual choices which now produce what is called the balance of demand (and therefore determine large areas of the curriculum) are necessarily influenced by public policy. Public policy is expressed through the hierarchy of institutions at the post-secondary level as well as at the secondary; through the teachers' reward systems; through the provision of buildings and equipment; through industrial training arrangements and the recruitment and training policies for public sector employees. Government action helps to distribute resources between different sections of the system, and so renders some parts more attractive than others.

A serious policy of curriculum development aimed at, say, shifting the balance of secondary education away from the arts and pure sciences and towards technology, would be futile if based entirely on the decisions of teachers at the school or subject level. It would need developmental decisions of a different order – for example, the designation of a few top university institutions as British MITs; a crash programme of teacher training in the applied sciences; examination reform; new salary scales for teachers of certain subjects; perhaps even a change in the student grant regulations to introduce differentials in favour of certain subject areas. It might involve the revival of the idea of specialist technical high schools, and the elaboration of new forms of apprenticeship and new forms of cooperation between schools and industry. The point is not to argue for any one of these items of possible policy; it is simply to suggest that a government which was serious about curriculum development would have to take decisions about the *system*, however reluctant it might be to intervene directly in the process.

Changing the context is not, in itself, enough. It is needed, not in order to replace other forms of development, but to give them meaning and direction. The necessary subject-based development must still follow – preparing the teaching materials, working out the arrangements for in-service courses, planning the introduction of new courses at the level of each particular school, and providing the appropriate supporting services. There is no circumventing the need to involve the individual men and women in the classroom, and to release their creativity and capacity to give expression to new ideas in terms of worthwhile school activities. There are still the awful warnings of the sterility of centrally imposed direction where it is unaccompanied by genuine development at intermediate levels and within the schools themselves. Nothing which we have written here should be interpreted as support for rigid curriculum controls imposed from on high; rather for better ways of reaching a collective view about curricular priorities which could then provide a framework within which creative development might take place.

There is every reason to welcome an altogether more positive approach to the management of the curriculum at the national and local level: an approach which pays as much regard to the wider context of education – the frame factors which determine the limits within which the schools must work – as has hitherto been devoted to course construction and subject-based development.

All this assumes that the public curriculum in some form or other continues to exist. It assumes that the schools still have a public role to play in transmitting such essentials of cultural unity as are necessary for even a plural society to cohere in some recognizable sense. To radical critics of schools and schooling that is, in itself, a conservative notion. For the de-schoolers the question to ask is not 'does the curriculum carry the particular body of knowledge, the particular attitudes and values which this society or that society wants to transmit?', but 'do we want schools to take this socially formative role at all?' So long as the argument is about what values the curriculum should convey – whether they be single or plural, overt or covert – it comes within the framework of a discussion of the public curriculum, and provides grist for the curriculum developer's mill. If, on the other hand, the professionalization and institutionalization of education is held to be inherently oppressive; if the education system is condemned because it is inextricably enmeshed in the corrupt validation of privilege and the certification of élite social groups; if, in short, schools and the idea of a public curriculum are rejected not only as instruments of social control but even as instruments of social liberation – then the public curriculum is altogether ruled out of court and curriculum development is subject to the same undiscriminating anathema as schools and schooling.

While politicians and professionals alike continue to ascribe social functions of one kind or another to schools, it is easy to resist the unreal choice posed by the de-schoolers between a public curriculum and no curriculum at all. But the more insistent questions are those which continue from year to year within the dynamics of the curriculum debate.

As the plural society evolves, the argument shifts – first one way and then the other – about the balance between the public and the private elements in the curricula which the schools provide: an argument which as much concerns the child-centred primary school teacher as it does the individualist parent who sees the curriculum simply in terms of equipping his child to compete more effectively in later life. These are questions which, by their very nature, cannot receive more than interim answers at any time. But they also raise issues which go beyond the competence of teachers as professionals, and demand answers from people and institutions which, in Britain at least, have allowed themselves to be excluded from the discussion.

Notes and references

Chapter 1 The curriculum and its development (pp. 11–20)

1. In *The Forum of Education*, Teachers' College, Sydney, Australia, July 1955.
2. Albert I. Oliver, *Curriculum Development*, Dodd Mead and Co., 1965.
3. See, for instance, W. Kenneth Richmond, *The School Curriculum*, Methuen, 1971. See also Lawrence Stenhouse, *An Introduction to Curriculum Research and Development*, Heinemann Educational, 1975, for a valuable discussion of the problem and purpose of definition, to which this chapter is indebted.
4. Robert Bell, *Thinking about the Curriculum*, Open University E.283, 1971.
5. See Geoffrey Caston, 'The Schools Council in Context', *Journal of Curriculum Studies*, 3, 1 (1971), pp. 50–64.
6. See D. W. Sylvester, *Robert Lowe and Education*, Cambridge University Press, 1974.
7. Joslyn Owen, *The Management of Curriculum Development*, Cambridge University Press, 1973.
8. The Education Act of 1944 underwrites this attitude. Part II, 7, declares that 'it should be the duty of the local education authority for every area, so far as their powers extend, to contribute towards the spiritual, moral, mental and physical development of the community . . .'
9. In an unpublished paper 'Defining the Curriculum Problem', 1972.
10. Eric Hoyle, 'How does the Curriculum Change?', *Journal of Curriculum Studies*, 2 (1969), reprinted in *The Curriculum: Context, Design and Development*, Open University, 1971.
11. See *Handbook on Curriculum Development*, Centre for Educational Research and Innovation (CERI), OECD, 1975, p. 13.

Chapter 2   A European perspective (pp. 21–34)

1. This chapter draws heavily on *Handbook on Curriculum Development*, CERI, OECD, 1975, to which the present authors contributed the opening section.
2. P. Dalin, *Strategies for Innovation in Education*, CERI, OECD, 1973, for a full discussion of the process of innovation and the relationship of curriculum development to other aspects of educational reform.
3. Sixten Marklund, *The Role of the Teacher in Educational Innovation in Sweden*, CERI, OECD, 1970.
4. Sixten Marklund and Eskil Bjorklund, 'National Council for Innovation in Education', in *Case Studies of Educational Innovation I: At the Central Level*, CERI, OECD, 1973.
5. Matts Håstad, Leif Svenson, Curt Oregbeg, *Some Facts about IMU*, Department of Educational and Psychological Research, School of Education, Malmö, Sweden, 1968.
6. Célestin Freinet, *Les Techniques Freinet de l'École Moderne*, Librairie Armand Colin, Paris, 1964.
7. Anne Corbett, 'Programme Control, French Style', *The Times Educational Supplement*, 4 February 1977.
8. Curriculum Design and Development, Unit 7, *The Child, the School and Society*, Open University E203, 1976, p. 128.

Chapter 3   Patterns of control (pp. 35–46)

1. Education Act 1944, section 68. The section reads: 'If the Minister is satisfied that any local education authority or managers or governors of any county or voluntary school have acted, or are proposing to act, unreasonably with respect to the exercise of any power conferred or the performance of any duty imposed by or under this Act, he may . . . give such directions as to the exercise of the power or the performance of the duty as appear to him to be expedient.'
   The Tameside case concerned the decision of an education authority in the Greater Manchester area not to introduce (in September 1976) the remaining stages of a comprehensive scheme. This scheme had been initiated by the Tameside authority under Labour control; in May 1976 control passed to the Conservatives. When the Conservatives decided to stop the scheme and retain some grammar schools and an eleven-plus selection procedure, the Secretary of State issued

a direction to Tameside to desist and carry through the previous scheme.

The House of Lords upheld a decision of the Court of Appeal, headed by the Master of the Rolls, Lord Denning, that the Secretary of State had inadequate grounds for concluding that the proposed action of Tameside was unreasonable. Tameside brought witnesses to show that some people who were (in the legal sense) reasonable, believed that what they had determined to do was defensible, and the Secretary of State failed to call evidence strong enough to rebut this. It was common ground between the two sides that the Secretary of State could not simply substitute his own opinion for that of Tameside. The Tameside judgment was important because it was evidence of the increasing willingness of the courts to examine the way ministers exercise powers given them under Act of Parliament.

2. Education Act 1944, section 23.

3. See Robin Auld, QC, *William Tyndale Junior and Infant Schools Public Inquiry* (Report to the Inner London Education Authority), ILEA, 1976.

4. Circular 113 (1946).

5. George Bruce, *Secondary School Examination – Facts and Commentary*, Pergamon Press, 1969.

6. By the early 1960s there were already counties and county boroughs where the number of O Levels obtained in secondary modern schools exceeded those obtained in the grammar schools. Of course the modern school population was three times that of the grammar schools, but the impact of the GCE in the modern schools was nevertheless highly significant, and one of the contributing factors behind the trend towards comprehensive schools. If the modern schools could organize effective O Level teaching, why was it necessary to distinguish, formally, between grammar and modern school children at eleven?

7. *Statement of Conditions of Recognition for Regional Examining Bodies, with Explanatory Notes* (Fifth Report of the Secondary Schools Examination Council), HMSO, 1962.

8. The constitution and committee structure of the Council, revised in 1968, reflected the belief that the teachers should have the majority voice on all curricular matters, while associating local authority representatives, assessors from the Department of Education and Science, representatives of the universities, industry and the trade unions in the work. Its senior staff has correspondingly been drawn from civil servants, HMIs, local authority administrators and

advisers, and from the ranks of practising teachers. Its chairman (appointed by the Secretary of State) has been chosen in rotation from the local authorities, the teachers' unions and higher education. The biggest single block of votes on the teachers' side has gone to the National Union of Teachers. Having power and responsibility in the Council, the NUT have used it – and in so doing have antagonized the DES and the local authorities.

Chapter 4   Agents of change (pp. 47–63)

1. Harold Nicolson, *Diaries and Letters 1939–45*, ed. Nigel Nicolson, Collins, 1967.

2. *Educational Policy and Planning – Sweden*, OECD, 1967.

3. See Maurice Kogan, *Advisory Councils and Committees in Education*, Routledge and Kegan Paul, 1974.

4. *The Education of the Adolescent*, HMSO, 1926.

5. *16 to 18*, HMSO, 1959.

6. *Children and their Primary Schools*, HMSO, 1967.

7. See E. C. Edmonds, *The School Inspector*, Routledge and Kegan Paul, 1962. See also a brief study by John Blackie, *Inspecting and the Inspectorate*, Routledge and Kegan Paul, 1970, and a DES pamphlet, *HMI Today and Tomorrow*, 1970.

For more extensive argument about the present and future role of the Inspectorate, see the *Report* of the Parliamentary Select Committee on Education and Science, session 1967–8, Part I, HMSO, 1968. This includes the evidence given before the Select Committee by a wide range of witnesses including the DES and the Inspectorate.

8. A classic example of how traditional curriculum development has worked can be culled from Janet Adam Smith's biography *John Buchan*, Hart Davis, 1965, p. 228. Following the publication in 1921 of the Report of a departmental committee on *The Teaching of English in England*, Buchan (then a director of Thomas Nelson, the Edinburgh-based publishers) persuaded Sir Henry Newbolt, who had chaired the departmental committee, to collaborate on a series of English texts intended to exemplify the curricular aims of the report.

9. For example, six English course books written by Ronald Ridout, and published by Ginn, sold a total of more than 1 250 000 copies in 1975–6. Arthur Abbott's *O Level Physics* (Heinemann) has sold 1 400 000 copies since 1963. W. F. H. Whitmarsh's *First French Book* (Longman) sold one million copies in its first twenty years.

Many of these sales were to overseas countries; but the figures also indicate a huge market in British schools.

Chapter 5   Subject-based developments (pp. 64–80)

1. Ronald G. Havelock, *Guide to Innovation in Education*, 1970, and *Planning for Innovation*, 1971, both published by the Center for Research on the Utilization of Scientific Knowledge, University of Michigan, Ann Arbor.
2. As earlier advocated by H. E. Armstong. See W. H. Brock, 'Prologue to Heurism' in *The Changing Curriculum*, History of Education in Society series, Methuen, 1971 (Armstrong's own exposition was set out in *The Teaching of Scientific Method*, Macmillan, 1903).
3. Clare Burstall *et al.*, *Primary French in the Balance*, NFER Publications, 1975.
4. *Evaluation in Curriculum Development: Twelve Case Studies*, Macmillan Education, 1973.
5. *Beyond the Stable State*, D. A. Schon, Penguin, 1971.
6. Célestin Freinet, *Les Techniques Freinet de l'École Moderne*, Librairie Armand Colin, Paris, 1969.
7. The matrix was first developed by Tony Becher for an OECD seminar on curriculum development at Illinois in 1971, and was reproduced in its present form in the published report of that seminar, *Styles of Curriculum Development*, Stuart Maclure, CERI, OECD, Paris, 1973.

Chapter 6   System-based development (pp. 81–90)

1. *Children and their Primary Schools*, HMSO, 1967.
2. See the report of the Bullock Committee, *A Language for Life*, HMSO, 1975, chapter 20.
3. Neville Bennett, *Teaching Styles and Pupil Progress*, Open Books, 1976.

Chpater 7   Fragmentation and integration (pp. 91–108)

1. The fullest exposition of Basil Bernstein's doctrine of classification and framing is given in vol. 3 of his *Class, Codes and Control*, Routledge and Kegan Paul, 1975.
2. The classic case against transfer was put by E. L. Thorndike in

'Mental discipline in High School Studies', *Journal of Educational Psychology*, **15**, 1 and 2 (1924), pp. 1–22, 83–98. A more recent statement of the case, based on the philosophy of knowledge rather than on cognitive psychology, is given in P. H. Hirst, *Knowledge and the Curriculum*, Routledge and Kegan Paul, 1974, especially chapters 2 and 3.

3. *The Times Educational Supplement*, 26 September 1975, 3 October 1975, 17 October 1975.

4. *The Whole Curriculum 13–16*, Evans/Methuen Educational, 1975.

5. L. C. Taylor, *Resources for Learning*, Penguin, 1971.

6. See the accounts by Virginia Makins in *The Times Educational Supplement*, 4 September 1970, 25 June 1971, 16 June 1972, 15 May 1975, 23 May 1975.

7. A comprehensive review of these possibilities, though concerned with higher education, is relevant to schools as well and is to be found in G. Squires *et al.*, *Interdisciplinarity*, Nuffield Foundation, 1975.

Chapter 8   Responsiveness to change (pp. 109–29)

1. Many of the ideas and allusions in this chapter are drawn from the excellent comparative study (undertaken for the Council of Europe, by Jean Rudduck and Peter Kelly, *The Dissemination of Curriculum Development*, NFER, 1976.

2. Marshall Heron, 'On Teacher Perception and Curricular Innovation', *Curriculum Theory Network*, Monograph supplement, 1971.

3. David L. Clark and John E. Hopkins, 'Roles for Research, Development and Diffusion', CRP Project Memorandum 1, 1966 (cited by Ronald G. Havelock in *Planning for Innovation*, CRUSK, University of Michigan, Ann Arbor, 1971).

4. Elihu Katz, Martin L. Lewin and H. Hamilton, 'Traditions of Research on the Diffusion of Innovations', *American Sociological Review*, **28**, 2 (1963), pp. 237–52.

5. Jean Rudduck and Peter Kelly, *The Dissemination of Curriculum Development*, NFER, 1976, p. 10.

6. *Dissemination and In-service Training*, Pamphlet 19, Schools Council, 1974.

7. A full account of the Project's dissemination strategy is given in Jean Rudduck, *Dissemination of Innovation: the Humanities Curriculum Project*, Evans/Methuen Educational, 1976.

8. Perhaps the most significant recognition of this possibility was in

the James Report (*Teacher Education and Training*, HMSO, 1972). The theme was developed in the 1972 White Paper, *A Framework for Expansion*, Cmnd 5174, HMSO – though its proposals were overtaken by economic events before any large-scale attempt could be made to implement them.

9. *Curriculum Development: Teachers' Groups and Centres*, Schools Council Working Paper 10, HMSO, 1967.

10. *Dissemination of Innovation: the Humanities Curriculum Project*, Jean Rudduck, Evans/Methuen Educational, 1976.

Chapter 9 Evaluating curriculum innovation (pp. 130–49)

1. Ralph W. Tyler, *Basic Principles of Curriculum and Instruction*, University of Chicago Press, Chicago, 1949.

2. Charles Silberman, *Crisis in the Classroom*, Random House, New York, 1970.

3. A good example of such a costing study is given in E. W. Hewton, 'Nuffield Mathematics 5–13: a profile', *International Journal of Mathematics Education in Science and Technology*, **6**, 4 (1975).

4. Michael Eraut, 'Some Recent Evaluation Studies' in *Curriculum Evaluation Today*, ed. David Tawney, Macmillan Education, 1976.

5. Malcolm Parlett and David Hamilton, 'Evaluation as Illumination', reprinted in *Curriculum Evaluation Today*, ed. David Tawney, Macmillan Education, 1976.

6. *Evaluation in Curriculum Development*, Macmillan Education, 1973.

7. Wynne Harlen, *Science 5–13: a Formative Evaluation*, Macmillan Education, 1975.

8. Michael Scriven, 'Pros and Cons about Goal-Free Evaluation', *Journal of Educational Evaluation*, University of California at Los Angeles, December 1972.

9. *Teachers' College Record*, **73**, 3 (February 1972).

10. Lawrence Stenhouse, *An Introduction to Curriculum Research and Development*, Heinemann Educational, 1975.

11. David Hamilton *et al.*, *Beyond the Numbers Game*, Macmillan, 1977.

12. Barry MacDonald, 'Evaluation and the Control of Education', in *Curriculum Evaluation Today*, ed. David Tawney, Macmillan Education, 1976.

13. The case for such a partnership is eloquently argued by

Lawrence Stenhouse in his *Introduction to Curriculum Research and Development*, Heinemann Educational, 1975.
14. Clare Burstall *et al.*, *Primary French in the Balance*, NFER Publications, 1975.
15. Barry MacDonald, 'Evaluation and the Control of Education', in *Curriculum Evaluation Today*, ed. David Tawney, Macmillan Education, 1976.

Chapter 10   The politics of acceptability (pp. 150–66)

1. *The Teacher, the School and the Task of Management*, Heinemann, 1973; *Authority and Organisation in the Secondary School*, Macmillan, 1975.
2. Its report was published under the title *The Whole Curriculum 13–16*, Evans/Methuen Educational, 1975.
3. *Enquiry 1: Young School Leavers*, HMSO, 1968.
4. Frank Musgrove and Philip Taylor, *Society and the Teacher's Role*, Routledge and Kegan Paul, 1969.
5. The William Tyndale affair is fully documented in the report of the inquiry carried out by Mr Robin Auld, QC, on behalf of the ILEA – *William Tyndale Junior and Infant Schools Public Inquiry* ILEA, 1976; and by John Gretton and Mark Jackson in *William Tyndale – a Collapse of a School or a System?*, Allen and Unwin' 1976.
6. See Leila Sussman and Gayle Speck, 'Community Participation in Schools: the Boston case', *Urban Education*, January 1973.

Chapter 11   The dynamics of the public curriculum (pp. 167–78)

1. For a lively but fiercely partisan account of Risinghill, see Leila Berg, *Risinghill: the Death of a School*, Penguin, 1968. See also a series of films made for Open University course E203 on 'Curriculum design and development', including *The Mackenzie File* produced by Ken Little; two films on Stantonbury – *Stantonbury, a blueprint*, produced by David Seligman, and *Myers Grove School*, produced by Caroline Pick.
2. Robin Auld, QC, *William Tyndale Junior and Infant Schools Public Inquiry* (Report to the Inner London Education Authority), ILEA, 1976.

Index